THE BOOK OF

THE BOOK OF

DAD

Dadication's What *You* Need!

Written by A Dad
(Paul Barker)

FOURTH ESTATE · *London*

First published in Great Britain in 2007 by
Fourth Estate
An imprint of HarperCollinsPublishers
77–85 Fulham Palace Road
London W6 8JB
www.harpercollins.co.uk

Visit our author blog: www.fifthestate.co.uk

1 3 5 7 9 10 8 6 4 2

A catalogue record for this book is available from the British Library

ISBN-13 978-0-00-725847-5

Book Design and Typesetting by
HarrimanSteel,
Studio 3.08,
56 Shoreditch High Street,
London, E1 6JJ
www.harrimansteel.co.uk

Illustration by Matt Blease

Printed in Great Britain by Butler & Tanner, Frome

For Bill

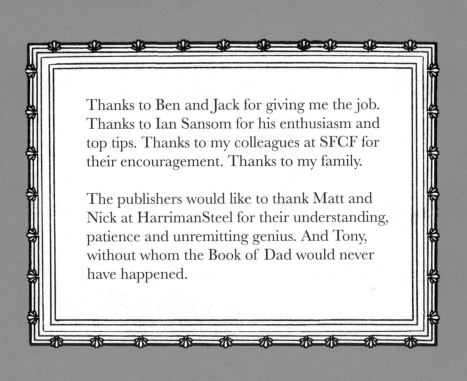

Thanks to Ben and Jack for giving me the job. Thanks to Ian Sansom for his enthusiasm and top tips. Thanks to my colleagues at SFCF for their encouragement. Thanks to my family.

The publishers would like to thank Matt and Nick at HarrimanSteel for their understanding, patience and unremitting genius. And Tony, without whom the Book of Dad would never have happened.

CONTENTS

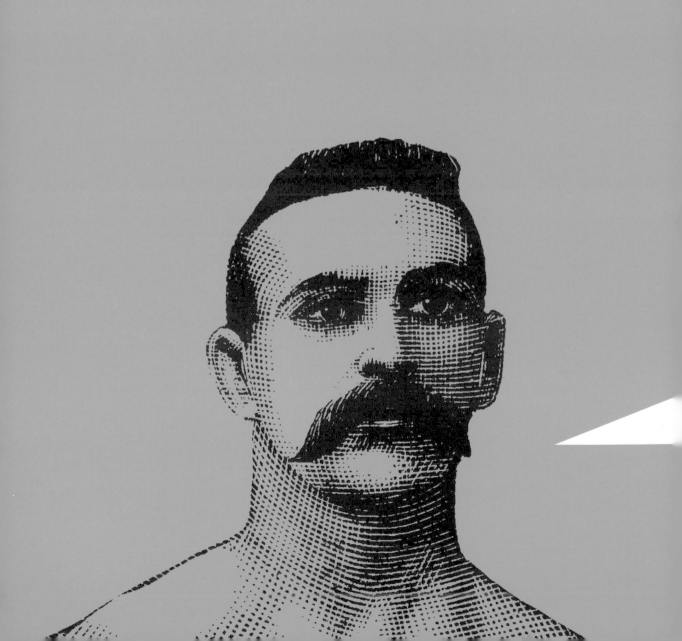

Foreword, Who is Dad?

Dad. Say it. Dad. What does Dad mean? Dad's not Father. No. Not Papa. Definitely not. Not Daddy, not Daddio. No way. Don't even consider Pater. Dad is something and someone else entirely. Dad. He has a solid monosyllabic quality, a comforting bluntness. Dad is all homely and informal in his open-necked shirt. Dad is unique and universal, a fascinating amalgam of qualities, vices and foibles. Dad is drama and excitement, unfolding action, comedy, romance, soap opera, game show. All human life is in Dad. Dad is a landscape and a portrait. Dad is history; Dad is culture. Dad reaches his arms around the world. Dad is a king with an invisible crown. Dad is the centre, gravity, the slowly spinning gyroscope from which all things come. Dad is all this and more. Pretty much.

You might be a Dad; you might not. But, whoever you are, rich or poor, black or white, great or small, man, woman or child, you will know how essential Dad can be. You will know of an occasion, an incident, an accident, something from your very own past that says something about the nature, the role, the purpose of Dad. Dad is part of nature's great cycle. Dads have children; children have Dads. And so on. It's time to celebrate Dad.

PART ONE

Know your Dad

Know Your Dad

Dads are, of course, people. For this reason, Dads and expressions of Dadness are infinitely varied. But, infinitely varied or not, they can be analysed and assessed, and many fall into recognisable patterns of behaviour. So, if you're trying to figure out exactly who and what your Dad is, or you are a Dad and you're trying to figure out exactly who and what you are, or you are a Dad and you know exactly who and what you are, but you're thinking of re-inventing yourself, then it's worth making brain-space for the types of Dad on offer.

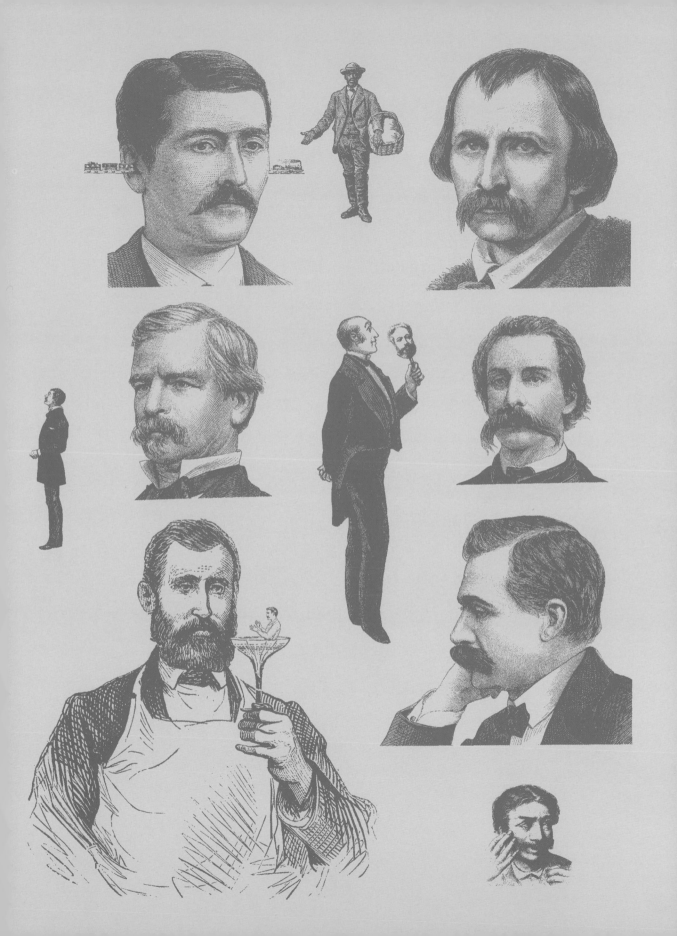

How Strict is Your Dad?

Your Dad finds the twelve-year-old you smoking a Woodbine in the potting shed. His response is to …

a) Enlist you in the navy.

b) Withdraw library privileges for a month.

c) Say, without looking at you, 'Woodbines are for the servants. You should have asked me.'

If you answered:

a) Your Dad is pretty strict. At least he lets you live.

b) Your Dad is pretty savvy – he knew you'd prefer a caning to get it over with.

c) Your Dad may not be your real father.

Dad Rule

Dads come in different levels of scariness – some can be tyrants, others are more like big cuddly toys you take money from. Some can fail to instil any morals at all.

How Fashionable is Your Dad?

Your parents are invited to a friend's fortieth-birthday bash. Your Dad wears …

a) That somewhat sombre suit he wore when he appeared before the Commons Select Committee.

b) His Rolling Stones Voodoo Lounge Tour T-shirt.

c) The ironed top and trousers your Mum put out for him.

If you answered:

a) Your Dad is not very fashionable, but it's okay because he really doesn't care.

b) The answer is the same.

c) Your Dad could possibly be quite … 'cool'. In this case it all depends on your Mother.

Dad Rule

There is a very general and very simple rule when it comes to Dads and fashion – they are not fashionable.

How Old is Your Dad?

You run to your Dad, new football in hand, and beg him to come outside for a game. Your Dad …

a) Has snatched the ball from you and has dribbled halfway down the garden before you have laced up your boots.

b) Lowers the *Daily Telegraph*, puts down his pipe and says, 'That's more of a weekend sort of thing, chum. I've been working, so I just want to read the obits, puff the old St Bruno and sip on a single malt. All right?'

c) Does nothing. But the nurse beside the bed puts her finger to her lips and shakes her head.

If you answered:

a) Your Dad is still plenty youthful and good for all the outdoor stuff.

b) Your Dad is probably past his peak, but good for the occasional outing. If you have two older siblings you are very likely an accident.

c) It sounds like you could be accidental or illegitimate. Either way, you're playing alone.

Dad Rule

Dads are not constrained by biology in the same ways that Mums are. There have been some famous octogenarian Dads with plenty to offer (mostly cash).

How Left Wing is Your Dad?

A man canvassing for an extreme right-wing party comes to the door. Your Dad …

a) Punches him on the nose.

b) Tries to punch him on the nose, but fails.

c) Says he doesn't believe in God, thank you very much, and closes the door.

If you answered:

a) Your Dad is probably more violent than ideologically committed.

b) Your Dad is probably committed but inept.

c) There are a number of possibilities, including the possibility that your Dad is highly committed but frequently drunk.

Dad Rule

Left-wing Dads are becoming increasingly rare. These days you are more likely to have a generally Anti-Capitalist Dad. If you have got the genuine article, treasure him – he's highly collectable.

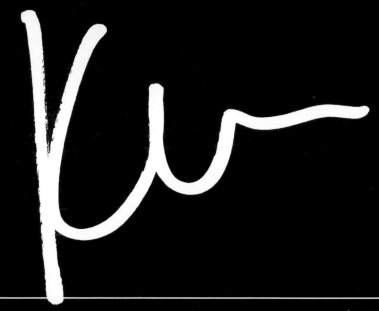

Ken – The silver fox, Ken smells of new and cheap leather sofas. An impressive covering of chest hair belies a sharp intellect and a lateral-thinking mind; perfect for the *Sunday Express* crossword. Myopic to the point of absurdity, Ken's glasses would happily withstand a lunar re-entry.

How Puerile is Your Dad?

The presenters of a wildlife TV programme are discussing 'a beautiful pair of tits'. Your Dad …

a) Sniggers his soup out through his nose.

b) Says, 'The one on the left looks a good deal more plump.'

c) Says, 'Yes.'

If you answered:

a) Your Dad is puerile, but only averagely so.

b) Your Dad is clearly highly suggestible and could be dangerous.

c) You are the proud possessor of an ambiguous Dad. Ambiguous Dads can be great fun.

Dad Rule

Generally speaking, a puerile Dad tends to be a bit irksome. Most Dads understand that puerility is immature and that's not what your kids want from you.

How Punctual is Your Dad?

Your Dad has an important meeting at 9 a.m. He …

a) Leaves an hour early in case the first train is cancelled or delayed.

b) Contributes to the meeting by mobile phone from the car park of a Little Chef.

c) Has his presentation available as a download from a dedicated Internet site, and is available for questions via live web-cam conferencing.

If you answered:

a) Your Dad is a sound, punctual man who takes his responsibilities seriously.

b) Your Dad may have good intentions, but he has no strategy.

c) Your Dad doesn't need to be punctual because he's living in the future.

Dad Rule

A punctual Dad is a good Dad – especially after football practice, the cinema, the school dance or a five-hour bender in a nightclub.

What Does Your Dad Always Carry with Him?

On the way back from a holiday in Devon, the family car breaks down at night on Dartmoor. Your Dad produces his …

a) Tool kit. He then busies himself under the bonnet for a couple of minutes before returning to the car, starting it first time and muttering, 'Thought so,' to himself.

b) SAS survival manual. He then gets everybody out of the car and begins the search for 'high ground and cover'.

c) Guitar. He then gives the family a heart-felt rendition of Warren Zevon's 'Werewolves of London'.

If you answered:

a) Your Dad is awesome and, even though he might spend much of his time in the garage, is definitely a handy Dad in a crisis.

b) Your Dad is probably fairly good in a sticky situation, but may overreact. A dogged, level-headed Mum helps in such cases.

c) Your Dad is really entertaining to have around, but may not be able to keep you alive in a mortal danger scenario.

Dad Rule

Most Dads carry something with them, whether a pen or a copy of Lyrical Ballads. It helps them feel ready for something.

How Philosophical is Your Dad?

The family is on a day trip to Tenby when a weirdo approaches in the street and tells your Dad that he is nothing more than a product of dominant ideology. Your Dad replies …

a) 'What do you mean by product? What do you mean by dominant? And what do you mean by ideology?'

b) 'I'm already a member, thank you very much.'

c) 'Er …'

If you answered:

a) Your Dad is probably a fairly philosophical fellow. At least he likes to settle the terms of reference.

b) Either your Dad doesn't like being stopped in the street, or he's agreeing with the terms of reference in an ironic sort of way.

c) Your Dad is probably not used to the cut and thrust of intellectual debate. He could still be a great guy though.

Dad Rule

A philosophical Dad is a good thing. Certainly he is more likely to understand any difficulties his children might have, rather than lashing out or shouting. Another good way of testing how philosophical your Dad might be is to keep asking 'why?' and see how long it takes him to lose his rag.

What Does Your Dad Call You?

Part One

Your Dad comes home from a lengthy business trip. You are playing in the street and see him turn the corner, his briefcase in his hand. You run towards him, and, beaming his most adoring smile, he opens his arms wide to receive you. He calls out …

a) 'Hey, Scout! Good to see you!'

b) 'Hey, little monkey!'

c) 'Hey, it's you!'

If you answered:

a) Your Dad is Gregory Peck in *To Kill a Mockingbird*. That's rare. It's also excellent, as Gregory Peck plays a highly heroic Dad in a film of a book in which a highly heroic Dad is a central character.

b) Your Dad sees you as something of a pet. At some point he will need disabusing of this idea.

c) Your Dad probably can't remember your name. If you are one of numerous siblings, this is what you are probably used to. If you are an only child and your Dad is often away on lengthy business trips, it's just possible that he's a bigamist, or at least living a double life.

Part Two

You have received an unusually poor school report and your Dad summons you to the study to reprimand you. He calls out …

a) Your full name. For example, John Prestatyn Erasmus Smith, or Emily Rosamund Mooncalf Jones.

b) (Depending on gender) simply 'Boy' or 'Girl'.

c) 'Yo, Loser!'

If you answered:

a) Your Dad is okay. He just wants you to see yourself as a full person, as someone who should have some self-respect, someone who should want to fulfil his or her intellectual potential.

b) Your Dad wants what Dad (a) wants, he just can't remember your name.

c) Your Dad takes a somewhat harsh attitude towards your accomplishments. Success *can* be achieved through fear of violent retribution, but it is a bit of an outdated approach.

Dad Rule

Sometimes what your Dad calls you can say more about him than you. Don't be afraid to tell him if you find your given moniker inappropriate. Sometimes he just might not see that 'Bell-end' is not a nickname all children will feel comfortable with.

How Financially Sound is Your Dad?

Your Dad comes into your room to 'talk about money'. He says …

a) 'You're twelve years old now, we need to discuss the corporation and your inheritance.'

b) 'You're twelve years old now, which is old enough to lend your old man some cash. I need some smokes and I got a tip from Newmarket.'

c) 'You're twelve years old now, so I'm giving you thruppence to put aside for your wedding.'

If you answered:

a) Your Dad is probably minted. This is a good thing, in that having nothing is certainly worse, but, as poor people hope, it won't guarantee your Dad happiness.

b) Your Dad is financially challenged. Unfortunately, this type of Dad often requires money as well as love, and rich and successful children are his favourite kind.

c) Your family may be the cast of a Dickens novel. So your Dad is basically a good man who has fallen victim to a cruel, unsentimental world.

Dad Rule

Let's face it, in any child's view, Dads are there to buy you things. So, the richer your Dad the better the things you get. It doesn't always work out, but the odds are not bad.

How Realistic is Your Dad?

You are a young child, and as the festive season approaches, you question your Dad about the existence of another father – Father Christmas. He says …

a) 'Of course Father Christmas exists. And if you've been a good child, I'm sure he'll bring you all the presents you want.'

b) 'Father Christmas is a myth. If you're going to ask me about God – ditto. Any more questions?'

c) 'Move out of the way. I'm watching the racing.'

If you answered:

a) Your Dad likes dreams and fantasy. These kinds of Dads tend not to be realistic, but are usually pretty indulgent.

b) Your Dad is one hard-nosed guy. He can seem harsh and uncaring at times and his children tend towards extremes – captains of industry or drug addicts.

c) Your Dad also likes dreams and fantasy. Unfortunately, these dreams are of a financial nature. Your Dad may be indulgent too, but not indefinitely.

Dad Rule

As with many Dad qualities, compromise is best. You want a Dad who is going to understand your dreams, even if they are genuinely stupid.

How Patriotic is Your Dad?

Your Dad is at an England–Germany game with some work colleagues. When the players are lined up and the band strikes up the national anthem, your Dad …

a) **Stands up and is suddenly surprised by a tear in his eye.**

b) **Turns to the Africa section of the *Economist*.**

c) **Slides his gaze along the line of players and shakes his head ruefully.**

If you answered:

a) **Your Dad is the common passive patriot. He gets emotional, but not often.**

b) **Your Dad is more committed to a bullish futures market than any particular country. This type of Dad is often rich, which is good, but don't expect him ever to let you win at anything.**

c) **Your Dad is looking to emigrate.**

Dad Rule

Patriotism is the last refuge of the scoundrel. Dads can be scoundrels, so don't be surprised if the old man has an inner flag-waver.

How Indulgent is Your Dad?

It's your eleventh birthday. As he hands you your present, he says …

a) **'I know how much you like whisky. I thought you should have some single malts of your own. You know, for when the guys are round and stuff.'**

b) **'Now we're quits.'**

c) **'Obviously, the personal butler is only a token. The real gift is in the card – I've listed the additions I've made to your stock portfolio.'**

If you answered:

a) **Your Dad is pretty indulgent. Single malts! What will your eighteenth be like?**

b) **You need to do some thinking. What did he mean? He certainly doesn't sound indulgent.**

c) **Your Dad may seem way too indulgent but it would seem you're already living a rarefied life, in which case you're probably already used to it.**

Dad Rule

An indulgent Dad may sound like a good thing. He is.

Where Did it All Begin?

Your earliest memory of your Dad is …

a) Him lying on a beach, a *News of the World* across his face and a strange noise coming from beneath it.

b) Him on TV, playing football.

c) Him coming home after being away for several months, and your mother crying and saying, 'You're alive!' over and over again.

If you answered:

a) Your Dad is just some guy. Makes you wonder why it is that *you* read the *Observer*.

b) Anything is possible – he may be running a pub in Oswestry by now, he may be the trainer of a string of Oaks winners.

c) It sounds like you are always going to be living up to something major.

Dad Rule

Your earliest memory of your Dad probably doesn't signify much. If it's good, then thinking about it from time to time might help re-enforce familial bonds. If it's bad, then let it go. It was probably just Dad on an off day.

So you think you know me?

PART TWO

The
Spotter's
Guide

The Spotter's Guide

Walk down any street, avenue, thoroughfare, mews or crescent, and you might well pass one. Buy an item in a shop or phone a hotline to complain about something, and you might well speak to one. Spill a pint in a public house and you might end up fighting one. Better still, get your binoculars and a pad and pencil and start spotting them. Dads. Like those finches that hang around the Galapagos Islands, Dads adapt to all sorts of environmental factors. Spotting and identifying these adaptations can almost make for a fascinating hobby or pastime. You might find that you know one. You might even find that you are one.

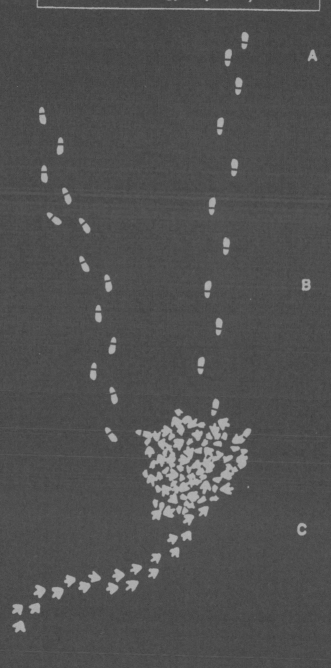

Dadology Mystery

Car Salesman Dad

Ideal Day

It looks like it's just going to be another slow Monday. But Car Salesman Dad knows that just around the corner is the big one, the once-in-a-lifetime moment, the moment when you look up from your desk and through the Portakabin window and see coming into the yard the kind of car you never see in a used-car lot.

A dishevelled pop star, of whom Car Salesman Dad has never heard, wants to sell his 1990 Rolls-Royce Silver Spirit in ocean blue, right now, for cash. In an instant he knows he can buy this car, and he knows someone who might want to buy it from him.

He suggests seven and a half to the pop star, who seems happy with eight, in cash, today. The test drive is sublime and the documentation is all good.

Just around the corner is the big one, the once-in-a-lifetime moment

By mid-afternoon, Car Salesman Dad has sold the Roller on eBay at a 400 per cent mark-up after he discovered just how famous the pop star actually was. So he's able to knock off early and go to pick the kids up from school. They take the scenic route home and have a celebratory fish-and-chip dinner.

Car Salesman Dad goes to sleep dreaming of cheques and pop stars.

Actual Day

In actuality, Car Salesman Dad sees no one all morning, spending his time polishing and sweeping and suchlike.

Two potential punters come in at lunchtime. One does nothing but shake his head and kick the vehicles, the other talks too much and it's soon apparent that that's what he wants – to talk.

When the kids get off school Car Salesman Dad foolishly gives them some keys so they can sit in the cars and pretend to drive them. He realises just how foolish when he looks up from his desk to see a 1998 Mondeo Ghia X lurching like a drunken kangaroo across the forecourt. All he can do is watch as it crunches into a low-mileage 2001 Volkswagen Polo automatic.

Nope, no airbags, but did I mention the heavy duty seatbelts?

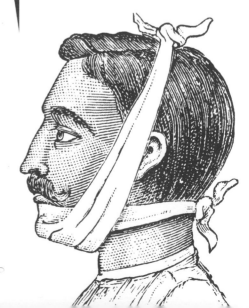

The children are sent home and the rest of the afternoon is spent down at the body shop having the panels beaten back and re-sprayed.

After dinner and a bath, Car Salesman Dad wants to do some paperwork, but is forced to spend the evening flat out on the sofa with bruised ankle, shin, knee, elbow and shoulder watching *Ground Force* with the wife after skidding and destroying his son's toy – an immaculate 1956 Dinky model Rolls-Royce Silver Spirit.

Oh crap, I'm off target!

Fashion

You have to have the suits. You can't sell anything without the suits. The suits say confidence and organisation and triumph and dreams come true. You can't sell a dream if you're not wearing a suit.

Transport

Car Salesman Dad takes his pick. He's never without an option. As long as it's cars. He doesn't do trains or bikes or taxis, even. He drives.

Snacks

Those boiled sweets in circular tins with powdered sugar on them. Pot Noodle for the Portakabin.

Life Expectancy

It's a high-pressure, big stakes game. These things take their toll. Just don't let it be too early. If there's something not quite right with the brakes get them checked before you borrow the car for a night out with the missus.

DAD noodle

Fried Breakfast Flavour

Journalist Dad

Ideal Day

A lengthy breakfast while reading the national papers and the international magazines is Journalist Dad's ideal start to the day.

Once the staying in touch is done the car comes to drive him into town. A few calls from the back seat to confirm the day's arrangements and firm up a few forthcoming assignments and interviews, and there is even time for a quick snooze.

After a light lunch with a moneybags film publicist at the Ivy, Journalist Dad gets a taxi to the Dorchester. His head and chest fill with hubris as he strides towards the desk to announce himself – here to interview Hollywood's goldenest of golden couples for... *Vanity Fair*. The golden couple radiate gilt-edged professionalism and all Journalist Dad has to do is admire their beauty and make sure the tape recorder is working. They happily autograph posters for the kids.

Once the staying in touch is done the car comes to drive him into town

In the evening, he has a couple of G&Ts at a Soho haunt and a good old brag with a few fellow freelancers, falls asleep on the car journey home, and bursts through the front door just in time to kiss the young ones goodnight, eat his dinner and fall sleep again in his armchair. Print it.

Actual Day

On a windswept morning in November, as he watches and takes notes on an unimportant game in the Anglesey Real Ale Sunday League, Journalist Dad is almost tempted to question his vocation.

More so when dogged defender Geoff 'the Bull' Maxwell's sliding tackle continues to slide across the sideline and into him, 'completely upending the hapless bystander'. At lunch he writes up the game, with a wet pencil on a wet pad, over a warm beer and wet sandwich at the pub.

In the afternoon, he interviews Anglesey's golden couple, the Stotts, who have moved their pig-slaughtering business to town and created 150 jobs, and who must therefore be referred to in only the most glowing of terms. They are boorish and ignorant, and it would take Shakespeare himself to write them up as even vaguely human. He describes them as 'charming and erudite' because they don't swear at him.

In the evening, whilst helping the kids with their homework, Journalist Dad realises that all three of his children, including his slack-jawed youngest, can spell better than him.

Sayings:

Totally off the record.

Are we talking exclusive?

Hold the front page, feral hoodie!

It's got to be in your handwriting.

Dogged defending.

Fashion

If you are the story, as celeb as the celebs you celebrate, you need to dress sharp. White shirts all the time is too newsy. A silk pastel and a quirky tie will get you into features, and into better parties.

If you are not the story, any old suit is okay, but it must be dark because it gets dirty with all the shinning up drainpipes and kneeling in front of letterboxes.

Transport

Journalist Dad has a second-hand car. It is probably a Volkswagen or a Saab. Something quirky is always good, a Fiat 500 perhaps, just in case you get a big scoop and someone wants to make a film about you.

Snacks

Pork scratchings and cigarettes. Cigarettes are snacks, aren't they?

Life Expectancy

There are Journalist Dads and there are Journalist Dads. One might investigate how drunk a wholesome media type gets at parties – he risks a punch on the nose.

Another might be looking into the activities of organised crime in major cities – he risks ending up entombed in a motorway flyover. The former is the greater danger but is less often fatal.

I love fags.

DCI Dad

Ideal Day

The ideal start to DCI Dad's day is being woken up by a 4 a.m. phone call. Here is a Dad who likes to hit the ground running.

Lots to mull over back at the station...

The streets are good and empty at this time of the day and, in a high-performance unmarked vehicle, he is at the scene in no time. A few PCs, two DCs and a DS are waiting for the DCI. There's a body, a weapon, a footprint and a tyre track – lots to mull over back at the station. The footprint and the tyre track point to a well-known local bad boy, but the DNA on the weapon suggests someone else.

DCI Dad has to bang his fist on his desk. If he doesn't get to say, 'Cuff the toe-rag. I know something you don't know and I'm gonna see you get twenty years for this' by boozer-opening time, someone's going to be sorry.

DCI Dad pulls his tie down a bit, works on a hunch and, after a brief car chase, brings in both the suspects. Sure enough, after a little loud sarcasm and some leaning forward on the desk, they both crack and cry like babies.

When he leaves the pub and goes home, he discovers DCI Mum telling one of the kids off for drawing on the walls. Although too drunk to get involved, DCI Dad amuses himself by shouting 'Book 'em, Dano!' before crashing, fully clothed, into bed.

Actual Day

Much of DCI Dad's morning is spent typing up notes and collating evidence and witness statements.

In the afternoon he appears in court. Much of this is sitting around, waiting and drinking grey coffee from a machine, while the case meanders and the judge interrupts. When he does finally get called, he realises that his pen has leaked in his pocket and green ink has spread across his chest.

All the defence lawyer tries to do is suggest that everything DCI Dad says is a lie, normally a weak strategy, but today it works. The case is thrown out.

Back home, tie down, he eats his dinner from a tray while he watches CSI, then finds he's out of fags and beer. In his desperation he resorts to stealing them from his eldest son's room.

When the light goes on, he is caught red-handed by DCI Mum, who then decides that this is the perfect time to sit him down and talk about his drinking problem.

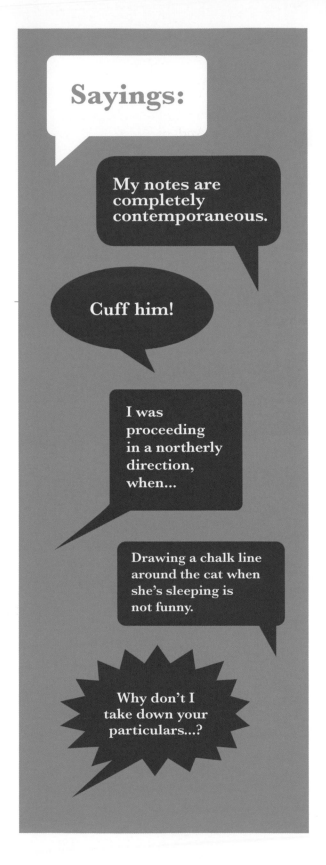

Sayings:

My notes are completely contemporaneous.

Cuff him!

I was proceeding in a northerly direction, when...

Drawing a chalk line around the cat when she's sleeping is not funny.

Why don't I take down your particulars...?

Fashion

Basically you have to get into plain clothes. That's the only way to look good in the force. Who looks cooler – Dixon of Dock Green or Frank Serpico? And, of course, a decent suit for court.

Transport

For work, a souped-up, red but dirty, Vauxhall Cavalier does the business. For the family, a souped-up, red but dirty, Vauxhall Cavalier estate does the business.

Snacks

Coffee and doughnuts followed by Nicorette gum and Red Bull. An unstoppable combo.

Life Expectancy

Here is a Dad who takes risks, who puts the world to rights and himself on the line. If he gets to retirement he's got a good pension lined up. Retirement for DCI Dad can be tricky.

His last day on the force is often his most hazardous and he may well find himself being shot. Better to climb the ladder. The life expectancy of a chief constable is higher.

Dangerous Pursuits Dad

Ideal Day

A good way to start the day dangerously is to have slept the night before in a hammock suspended thirty feet up a tree, and to wake with your family around you in their hammocks.

Another reason for this is that Dangerous Pursuits Dad and family are trekking into the Venezuelan forest to find La Mine de Satan, The Devil's Pit. The family is part of a larger party, intent on parachuting into the massive hole.

It is an awesome experience to stand on the precipice above the huge jungle abyss with your four-year-old daughter strapped to your chest. The jump is sublime – straight into darkness, and, when the chute opens, a slow drift down through a cool cave alive with shrieking birds and giant fruit bats.

Dangerous Pursuits Mum follows them down with the toddler.

The seven-hour hike back to the camp is well worth it and tires the kids out

The seven-hour hike back to the camp is well worth it and tires the kids out. By the time they have eaten their barbecued armadillo and sung a few campfire songs, all the family are ready for an early night in the hammocks.

Actual Day

What with it being a Sunday, and Dangerous Pursuits Mum wanting him out of the house so she can repair the zip-wire that runs from the parental bedroom to the shed, Dangerous Pursuits Dad takes the kids down to the recreation ground.

The youngsters love the rec because of the extensive monkey bars, and they waste no time monkeying all over them, as sure-footed as mountain goats. Dangerous Pursuits Dad has been thinking about the far corner of the climbing frame, which he calls The Old Man's Needle, and reckons that from this point it should be possible to get a couple of ropes across to the top of the slide, and climb over without having to touch the ground or step up via the roundabout. It's never been done; nor will it be done today.

While trying to remember what it is Dangerous Pursuits Mum told him to get for lunch on the way home, he misses his footing and falls off the kerb. He grazes his knees, shins, elbows and ears, and sprains his ankle. Walking is almost impossible.

Dangerous Pursuits Dad spends the rest of the day on the sofa, watching *Cliffhanger*, while the kids run up the stairs, zip-wire down to the shed, run up the stairs again, and so on.

Ouch.

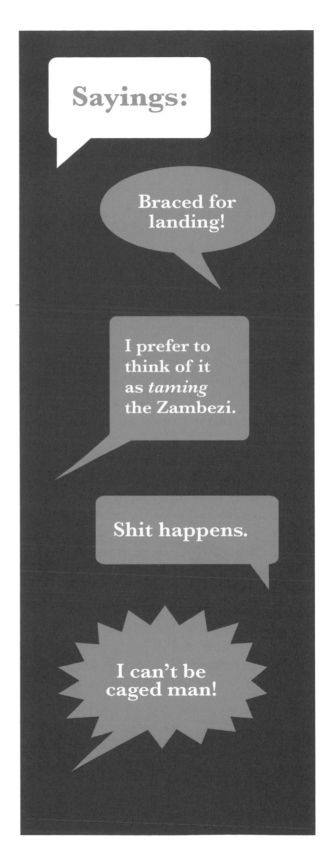

Sayings:

Braced for landing!

I prefer to think of it as *taming* the Zambezi.

Shit happens.

I can't be caged man!

Brian – A name synonymous with the colour
brown. A pipe smoker, a cord wearer and a
Volvo driver, Brian is not at home to Mr Danger,
or for that matter Mr Interesting, Mr Funny
and certainly not Mr Tickle. Brian scores high
on longevity, conformity, stability and low on
perversity, sociability and sperm count. In the
big scheme of things Brian just doesn't matter.

Retired Dad

Ideal Day

At 6 a.m. the clock radio comes on. Retired Mum likes Radio 5. Retired Dad goes downstairs and makes tea to bring back to bed. The couple breakfast in the kitchen, sharing toast and jam and bits of the *Daily Mail*.

In the morning they take the bus down to the golf course and play a round with retired friends. Lunch is a sandwich at the club and then it's off on the bus again to the local bowls club for a couple of games. Afterwards there is time to walk to the shops and stock up on sherry and toffee ice cream.

After an early supper, two daughters-in-law come round with the grandchildren. The little ones crash around, bouncing off the furniture and, much to Retired Dad's displeasure, eating great canyons through the ice cream tubs. When they leave, after fifteen minutes, he is happy and invigorated, but pleased that the invigoration stops there.

Mum turns off the TV and gives Retired Dad a look

In the evening, Retired Mum watches *Who Wants to Be a Millionaire?* and *Holby City*, while Retired Dad sits at his new computer typing up the letters of commendation he received before retirement and researching his family on the Internet.

When the engraved carriage clock chimes ten, Retired Mum turns off the TV and gives Retired Dad a look.

Actual Day

At just before 6 a.m. Retired Dad is woken by an unfamiliar moaning sound. In the next moment, grandchild number three appears in the doorway and announces that grandchild number two is being sick. Grandchild number three seems unaware that her own face is covered in red spots.

The morning, with the planned bus trip to the club to show the little ones how to play golf now long abandoned, is spent on three different buses getting to the doctor's.

Grandchild number three is sick on bus one; grandchild number two is sick on bus three. On the way home, diagnosis confirmed, immediate containment recommended, grandchild number two is sick on bus one, grandchild number three on bus three.

Despite the fact that Retired Dad tries to leave much of the coping to Retired Mum, the afternoon is spent in a darkened room reading children's stories, spooning soup, re-dampening flannels and emptying bowls of sick. Eventually the patients' proper care-givers turn up from their week away skiing in the Swiss Alps, relieving the shattered Retired Dad and Retired Mum.

After dinner and a quick sherry or two they collapse into their chairs. Retired Mum gets morose because she doesn't know any of the answers on *Who Wants to Be a Millionaire?* and one of her favourite *Holby City* characters is killed off.

The wheels on the bus go round and round, all day long!
SShh! Gran, you're embarrassing me!
THE BOOK OF DAD
BUY IT NOW! ESPECIALLY IF YOU ARE LOOKING AT THIS IN A BOOKSHOP!

Sayings:

Better take a coat – it might turn cold.

Take it easy, love.

Bowls is a bit more dynamic than people think.

Sherry?

When the carriage clock chimes wake them both at ten, Retired Dad realises that discovering on the Internet that his great-great-grandfather was a famous naval surgeon was just a dream.

Fashion

Just because you are retired there is no reason to let standards slip. A tie and a jacket, ironed trousers, polished shoes and the like – you have to keep it all going. You don't want to start falling apart like the Clarks at number 57.

Transport

Buses are free. What else is there to say?

Snacks

You might think Werther's Originals, but Refreshers and Spangles are surprisingly popular.

Life Expectancy

Technically, of course, Retired Dad could be a multi-millionaire in his forties. Probably not though. Retirement Dad's life expectancy depends on who he was. His territory is too wide. If you have hit retirement, you are already doing pretty good.

Keep it Real

New Age Dad

Ideal Day

Before a homemade organic muesli and wholemeal toast breakfast, there is time to do some yoga and meditation with the kids. The drive to school is beautifully peaceful, as New Age Mum and the nippers are all successfully denying the self and listening to the whale song.

The rest of the night is given over to several hours of tantric sex

New Age Dad has a good day at the health-food shop, as several customers are prepared to talk spiritually and holistically when buying their extra-large tubs of Hi-Performance Glutamine Weight-Gain Capsules. Lunchtime is sunny, and he meditates in the park.

In the evening, after fasting through teatime to gain greater spiritual enlightenment, the kids read out passages from the Bhagavad Gita and New Age Mum practises on Dad for her acupuncture exam.

Once the children are tucked up in bed, the rest of the night is given over to several hours of tantric sex.

Actual Day

Everyone oversleeps because the solar-powered alarm clock didn't go off. There is no time for any yoga, which makes New Age Dad feel his age, and the kids use it as an excuse not to make muesli but to have honey-frosted crunchies as an emergency breakfast.

The electricity bill arrives. It is big, and therefore bad in both financial and ecological terms. No one seems able to deny the self on the journey to school and he has to really crank up the whale song to pacify the youngsters.

The only customers at the health-food shop that day are young men with no necks asking if he sells steroids. He tries meditating at lunchtime, but it rains and he can't get the electricity bill out of his mind.

The wild rice and water chestnut dinner is nice, but the kids are getting less prepared to do spiritual readings, preferring instead to lock themselves away and watch soap operas. New Age Dad's chi is so out of balance that he has to have a Nurofen and half a bottle of Chianti to get rid of his headache.

He takes another Nurofen after New Age Mum has practised her acupuncture.

When I was your age I had eight jobs and five stomach ulcers!

Pushy Dad

Ideal Day

On a good day, the kids are up first and doing some practice. A nutritional breakfast sets them up well for the day and it's off to school early enough to get some more practice in before lessons start.

At lunch Pushy Dad nips out of the office to ring the kids to discuss that morning's lessons. He takes a full briefcase and leaves the office early so he can run them to their various after-school pursuits.

During the evening meal they discuss how the day went, using the subheadings: Expectations, Goals, Outcomes, Achievement, Progression and the General Plan. The big bonus of the day is that the local paper features all three of his children for their various achievements, two of them pictured.

Even on an ideal day, Pushy Dad has to work late into the night to finish the paperwork he brings home. But it's worth it, as he tiptoes up the stairs in the darkness, to hear one of them crying out from a dreaming sleep, 'The only time you'll find success before work is in the dictionary.'

Actual Day

The kids are so exhausted that they are difficult to rouse. Even repeating the Five Statements for a Successful Day fails to get them going.

They arrive at school early enough for practice, but he sees them scuttle to the far side of the playground, where they stand around texting. When he tries to call them at lunch for a progress report, they are unavailable.

In the afternoon an important meeting is extended and the kids have to get the bus to practice. Pushy Dad feels the loss of an opportunity to discuss the day's GCSE physics lesson with his son.

When he finally gets home there is much debate about how the kids managed to miss the bus to practice. During the evening meal no one wants to talk and he feels the vast abyss of disappointment opening beneath him.

As he climbs the dark stairs to bed, he counts off the Five Statements for a Successful Day, realising that none of them has been realised.

Fashion

The Pushy Dad isn't really concerned about fashion. You need a suit for awards ceremonies, but that's about it.

Transport

The Volvo 240DL estate is what you need. Rugged and reliable and plenty of space for sports kits, double basses, etc.

Snacks

Thorntons white chocolate champagne truffles.

Life Expectancy

The truth is that the life expectancy of the Pushy Dad can be affected by stress. Still, death tends not to come until (but soon after) he has witnessed his progeny's great achievement. Sometimes on TV, from his deathbed.

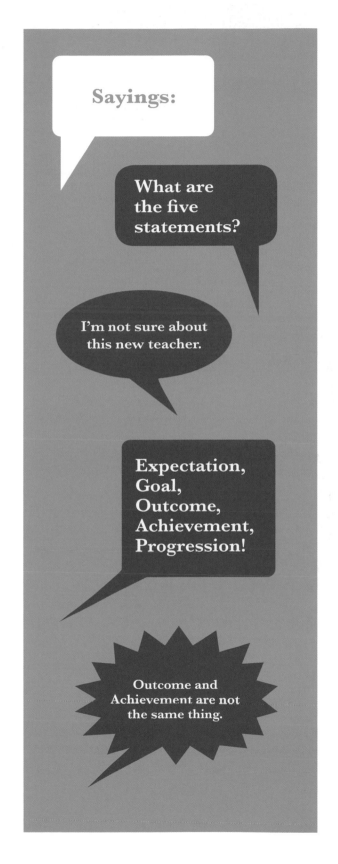

Sayings:

What are the five statements?

I'm not sure about this new teacher.

Expectation, Goal, Outcome, Achievement, Progression!

Outcome and Achievement are not the same thing.

$$D^2 = \frac{1}{c}\frac{1}{\ell}\frac{dl}{dt} = \frac{1}{c}\frac{1}{P}\frac{dP}{dt} \qquad OPC = \qquad \text{(knife)}^{53}$$

$$A^2 = \frac{1}{P^2}\frac{P_0 - P}{P} \sim \qquad 1 \qquad = (\text{GUARDIAN})^{(1a)}$$

$$D^2 = \frac{Kg}{3} + \text{(cloud)} + \text{(suitcase)}^2 = \qquad ^{(2a)}$$

Teacher Dad

Ideal Day

Of course teaching is a vocation and he's never 'off duty'. Equally the ideal day for Teacher Dad is one of his many holidays.

After a fish-and-chips supper, the family goes to see the new Pedro Almodovar film

So, after a fry-up at the B&B, they head down to the beach. Teacher Mum and Teacher Dad can sit in deck chairs and read the *Guardian* and *Telegraph* respectively, while keeping an eye on the young ones' unstructured learning time. They are building a sandcastle. Their construction does credit to their scholarly upbringing.

They are able to draw on a variety of fields of learning and combine them effectively in a clearly defined system of inter-relations. Meaning that the boy builds a mini-reservoir to solve the drainage problem with his moat, while the girl opts for some gothic castellation because it would 'attract chivalrous knights'.

After a fish-and-chips supper, the family goes to see the new Pedro Almodovar film. On the walk home the kids discuss the film with just a little prompting from Teacher Dad.

They all go to bed tired, happy and having learned something.

Actual Day

An actual day though, naturally, is spent working. Much of that working is managing OPC – other people's children. And other people's children are a rum bunch.

As he stares out of the window while the pupils work their way through the first five equations on page 22 before checking the working out with a neighbour, or while they score their names into the desks with flick-knives and shoot holes in the curtains with air pistols, Teacher Dad does some maths of his own – years, months, weeks, days, hours, minutes and seconds to retirement.

He has to stay behind for parents' evening. The canteen has laid on a slab of cheese-like material and a radish on a paper plate covered with cling film. The parents are distraught, resigned, accusatory, bewildered, indifferent and insane in equal measure.

He marks homework and eats a sandwich

By the time he gets home the kids are in bed. He marks homework and eats a sandwich. Teacher Mum goes to bed too. He joins her once he's prepared tomorrow's lunches and packed the kids' bags.

He finds a flick-knife in his son's satchel, which sends him to bed tired, unhappy and afraid he's learned something.

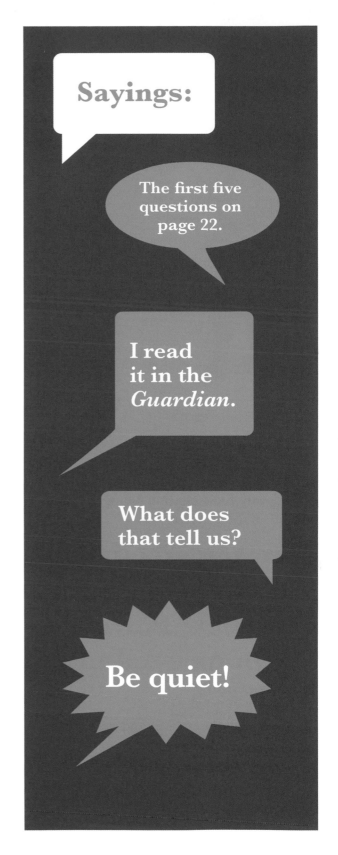

Sayings:

The first five questions on page 22.

I read it in the *Guardian*.

What does that tell us?

Be quiet!

Actual Day

The day starts with the trek to the country. Today there are three auctions simultaneously, so the family has to split up, which means that the children are not to bid on anything they find without consulting Antiques Dealer Dad first.

Dad had already got into a stupid macho bidding contest with a local dealer who spilled his wife's thermos

What this means in practice is that the kids never re-appear, and when they are collected they have with them some Nazi memorabilia – daggers, cap badges, SS armbands and the like, seven Edwardian dolls in various stages of decay and what was sold as the fossil of an early shrew-like mammal but is quite clearly only painted on to the rock.

And Dad had already got into a stupid macho bidding contest with a local dealer who spilled his wife's thermos. The result of which was his paying well over the odds for a bit of Spode. The journey home is spent silently calculating the cost.

I feel old.

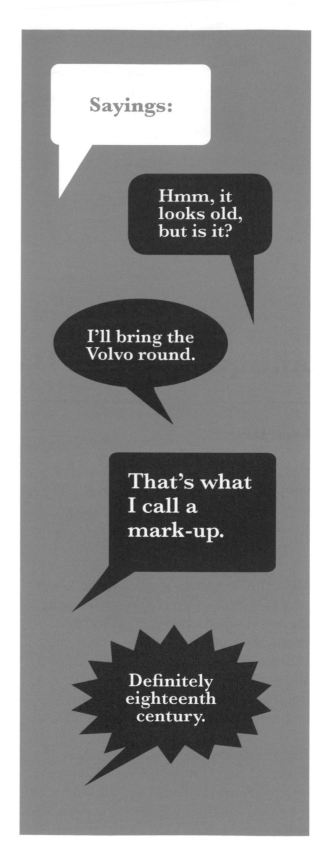

Sayings:

Hmm, it looks old, but is it?

I'll bring the Volvo round.

That's what I call a mark-up.

Definitely eighteenth century.

Fashion

You do have to look the part. You are selling, wheeling and dealing with class and the past. So you have to look a bit behind the times and a bit like a toff.

The ideal combination is brown brogues, fawn corduroy trousers, a green, fine-knit lamb's wool crew-neck jumper and a yellow silk cravat. Outdoors, add a Barbour jacket and a tweed flat cap. Suits and ties are for art dealers.

Transport

The Volvo 240DL wagon is without equal in the eyes of the antiques community. Antiques Dealer Dad would only be letting himself down if he drove anything else. It's rare to find a piece of furniture you can't get in the back.

Snacks

Bournville. Green and Black's 85% Dark. Toffoes or Everton mints in emergencies.

Life Expectancy

The thing about all that fancy stuff – the furniture and paintings, the lamps, the jewels, the commodes – is that it encourages ideas of grandeur. Antiques Dealer Dad can be a bit red of cheek if he's not careful.

He does tend to live at least until he has seen the ordinary and average from his own childhood become desirable and collectable and highly valuable.

Objection, baby!

Lawyer Dad

Ideal Day

Wednesday 10 a.m. The Old Bailey.

Lawyer Dad, Queen's Counsel Dad no less, listens to the sensuous sliding sound of his silks as he reaches forward to undo the spring-loaded catches of his black leather Aspinal briefcase and take out his files.

Today is a day of great, table-turning drama. Today is the day that will change the course of this trial definitively. He is the only one who knows this. People's lives are in his hands. He is going to use his intellectual powers to see that the cause of justice is furthered, to show the gallery, press and public, that the truth, should sufficient funds be forthcoming, will out.

After a few minor points with a minor witness, beautifully lulling all assembled into a state of mild torpor, Lawyer Dad surveys his stage, smiles jovially and calls for witness X. A brief hubbub circles the room, dissipating with the arrival of the

He hears the rustle of the silk once more...

surprise witness. With the right coaxing and encouragement, witness X's testimony electrifies the gallery, the jury box, the judge and the defence team.

As witness X leaves the witness box, still wiping tears from her eyes, the accused looks defeated, the jury look deeply moved, nodding at each other, and the judge gives

Lawyer Dad a brief but significant glance. He hears the rustle of the silk once more.

He might even be home in time for a game of cricket in the garden with children A and B.

Actual Day

Thursday 4.30 p.m. Bracknell Magistrates' Court.

Lawyer Dad, after finally managing to undo the stupid catch on the briefcase he bought from the Sue Ryder shop, reaches in to take out his brief. He shouldn't be here. He is standing in for a sick colleague.

It takes him several minutes to realise he's looking at the wrong files and he has to resort to spilling his case and the paperwork on to the floor in order to get the right file without looking as though he's a total fool. The other lawyer and the magistrate look suspicious.

The claimant – his dog dug up my flower beds and urinated on a child's bike – is not pleased to be represented by a stranger and the proceedings descend into a slanging match between two mad neighbours.

When the magistrates wade in with their judgement just to get the shouters to shout no more, they reserve a little segment of their conclusion to give Lawyer Dad a ticking off for his inept performance.

When he goes home, the horticultural dog owner tries to attack him and he has to lock himself in his car to avoid a bashing. At home he sits in his chair and prepares his papers for the next day, while Lawyer Mum and the kids watch re-runs of *LA Law* on TV.

When all the family is in bed, he lays down his paperwork, gets out the *Rumpole of the Bailey* video and goes to sleep dreaming he's Leo McKern.

Small service is true service, while it lasts.

Sayings:

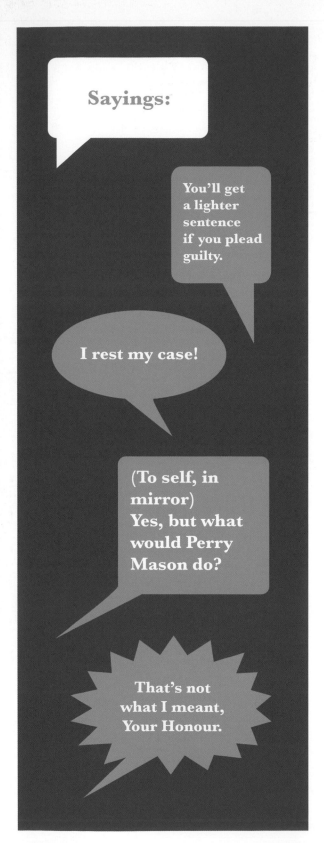

You'll get a lighter sentence if you plead guilty.

I rest my case!

(To self, in mirror)
Yes, but what would Perry Mason do?

That's not what I meant, Your Honour.

Fashion

Lawyer Dad aspires to one of the crazier fashion anachronisms. In sartorial terms, he harkens back to the seventeenth century. He likes wigs and gowns, pantaloons, black socks, big-buckled shoes. He's a role-player.

Transport

It's okay to start with a bicycle, but it should be taxis eventually. And a nice big German car for days out en famille.

Snacks

Cold packets of crisps from the machine.

Life Expectancy

Life expectancy is good. Very few are the Lawyer Dads who have been murdered by a client. The best possible healthcare is available once the hospital realises what Lawyer Dad is.

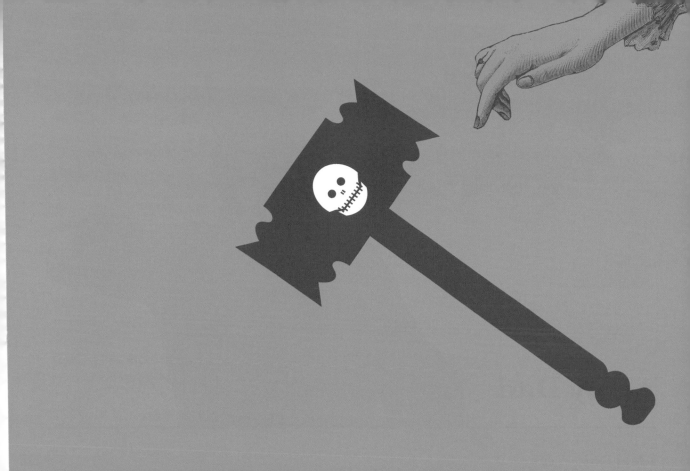

Agh! She Who Must Be Obeyed!

Sayings:

Pays to be a winner, now back you go again, sir.

Put that light out!

Damn You! Goddam You! Nobody D.O.R.'s after eleven weeks! Nobody!

The chain of command is there for a very good reason, young lady.

Fashion

Khaki. What else is there?

Transport

When the chips are down, only a Land Rover will give you the flexibility and toughness you need.

Snacks

Mars Bar. You can sing the song from the ad while you march.

Life Expectancy

The life expectancy of an Army Dad depends on how often he is on active service. In recent years life expectancy has declined a little.

Oh brother, I think I pulled my back again.

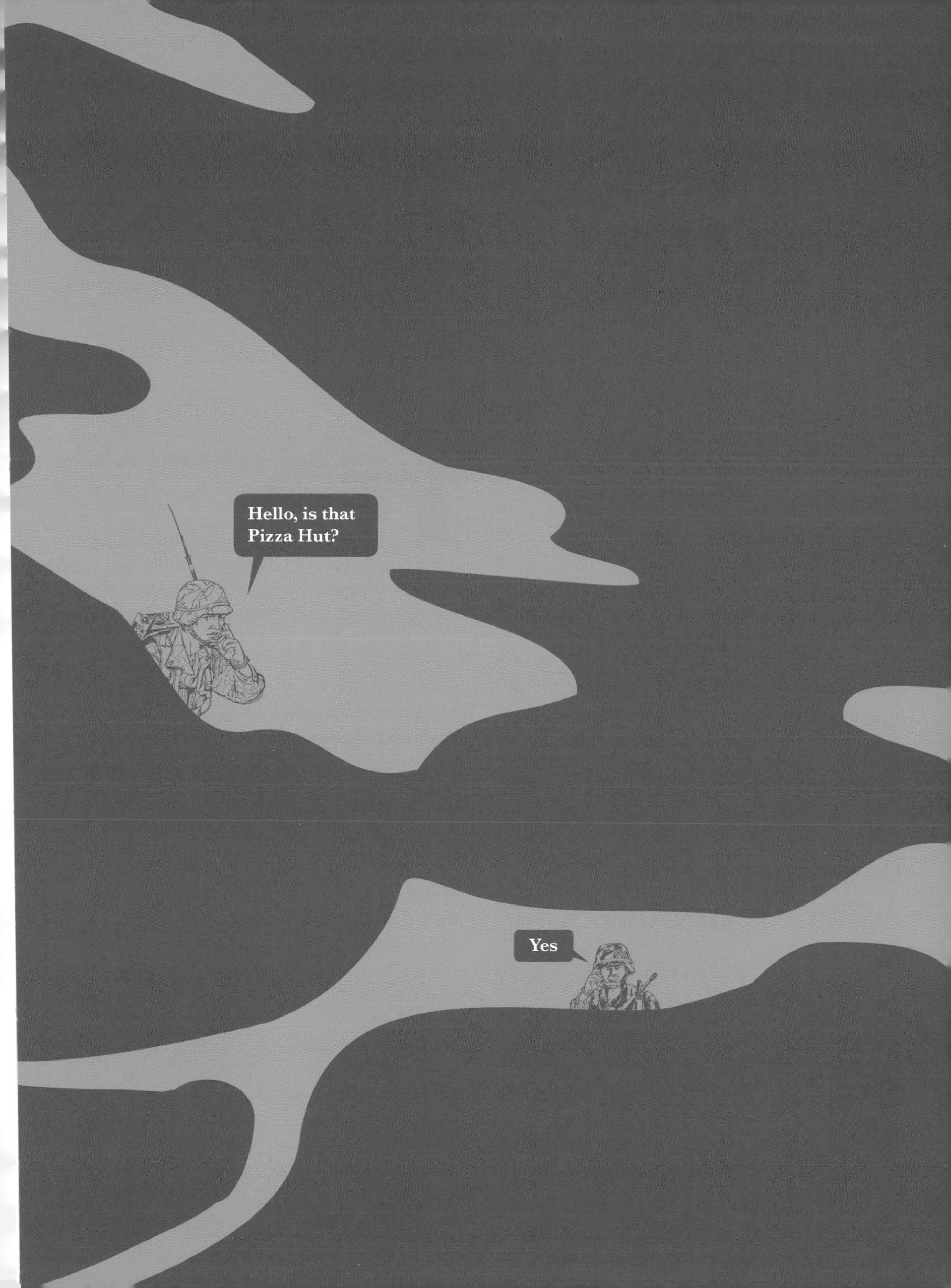
Hello, is that Pizza Hut?
Yes

Inventor Dad

Ideal Day

The sun is shining, the birds are singing in the trees and the only place to be is in the shed.

The hours spent working on the new flanges have paid off, and they turn out to be a precision piece of home engineering. The formula for the advanced polymer, unstable though it might have been for a while, looks like it might work at last. But the headline-grabber will surely be the successful development of the luminous lab coat, an idea so simple, so useful, so eco-friendly, that all the world will want it.

Inventor Dad comes back down the garden to the house beaming and glowing with self-belief and success. At dinner he makes the kids roar with laughter because he says things like, 'Hamish, if you don't eat your broccoli I know a pro-particle sema-bot that will!'

Inventor Mum knows that Dad is off to the Patent Office in the morning and they celebrate by firing up the newly completed Hypergasmofoggatronic.

Actual Day

The sleet is falling for a fifth consecutive day and an icy wind is piercing every crack in the shed's ageing woodwork. Water has dripped from the roof on to the stage-four plans and the measurements are illegible.

The flanges are missing and the cat has eaten the new polymer, a highly unstable compound, and is stuck to the door. To cap it all, the luminous lab coat, which seemed so promising, has hit a problem. Working with it in the shed seems to be giving Inventor Dad one heck of a tan.

When he goes back to the house he is cold, wet and despondent but glowing nonetheless. Inventor Mum tells him he'll soon be on the cover of *OK!* Magazine just by dint of his extreme orangeness.

He doesn't say much over dinner and all the family know that tomorrow is not a Patent Office day. Tomorrow is a shed day.

Fashion

For inventing there is a choice – either the lab coat, bought as a student, but still perfectly serviceable; or there is the boiler suit, bought for that first job at ICI all those years ago. Inventor Dad does have a suit. It's brown, and there's a brown tie to go with it. The suit is worn for trips to the Patent Office.

Transport

The bicycle. It's still a magnificent machine and a superb means of maintaining fitness. The train for trips to the Patent Office.

Snacks

Gobstoppers, lollipops, Fox's Glacier Mints. Anything that will last through those long hours in the shed.

Life Expectancy

Inventor Dads can go on for years. They are curious, optimistic and tenacious. Just the qualities needed for a damn good innings. A minority are lost to explosions, electrocution, radiation poisoning or madness, but, on the whole, the odds are good.

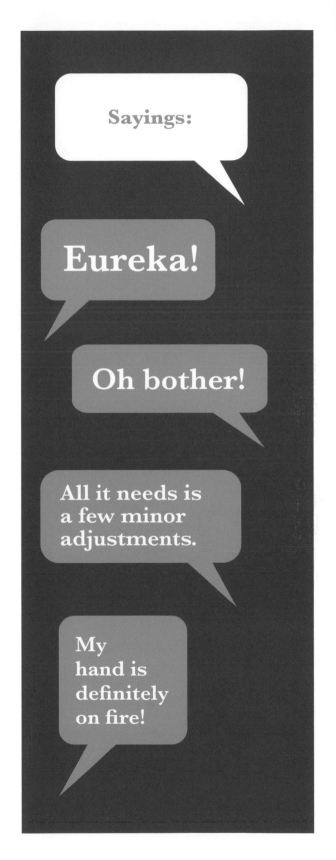

Sayings:

Eureka!

Oh bother!

All it needs is a few minor adjustments.

My hand is definitely on fire!

PART
THREE

D

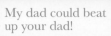

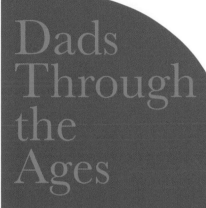

Dads
Through
the
Ages

Dads Through the Ages

Modern Dad doesn't know he's born. So says Post-War Generation Dad. And, of course, in some ways this is merely another familiar remark in the generational conversation that has been going as long as Dads themselves. But Modern Dad really does maintain a strikingly privileged position in comparison to his historical counterparts. Modern Dad has parental powers undreamed of by his forbears. Things like Disney videos and CBeebies. But it wasn't always so.

I really must fire my stylist!

Neanderthal Dad

While Neanderthal Dad may not have had Xboxes, My Little Pony or even school to divert the children, the pace of life was slower and the children less demanding. But with no school, it falls to Dad to make sure the youngsters learn how to make spears and stone axes, how to kill and skin animals, how to make fire, how to defend your cave from wolves and bears. So there's always something to do.

Neanderthal Dad takes the free-range approach to parenting. Without the threat of social services, the kids are allowed to roam wild in the ample backyard. Until hunting time that is, when they can come in jolly handy in baiting the sabre-tooth tigers and other nasties. Neanderthal Mum might not approve, but a few aggrieved grunts is easy enough to ignore.

What really keeps Neanderthal Dad and his large brain warm at night is his big idea. The big idea is for his daughter, who is not at all bad looking for an early proto-human, to get together with one of those new Cro-Magnon men. They're one heck of a sophisticated bunch.

Without the threat of social services, the kids are allowed to roam wild in the ample backyard

Mythic Hero Dad

With Mythic Hero Dad anything can happen. But whatever does happen, it's sure to be an adventure.

School isn't really an issue when you're out for the day challenging demigods

No, never a dull moment for this Dad's kids. School isn't really an issue when you're out for the day challenging demigods or fighting off minotaurs, harpies and sirens.

Besides, Dad's too busy taking care of business himself to worry too much about what the kids are up to. He's got enough

on his plate with appeasing tyrant kings, bare ankle shooting and cleaning out stinky stables. Sometimes, there just aren't enough hours in the day.

If the children do go off to work with Dad, they won't be seeing too much of Mum. She's staying at home and being the epitome of fidelity and belief. She needn't worry, though, because the kids will be regularly tested and learn in their own fashion. Quests and trials are not unlike coursework and exams.

We are the Romans!

Roman Dad

Why should Roman Dad need ASBOs or Ritalin to keep his children in check? He has gladiatorial combat, chariot races and lions eating Christians to keep them attentive and off the streets.

There's so much to do with them and no social workers telling you that you can't

It's a free for all! Ancient Rome is a great place to bring up children. There's so much to do with them and no social workers telling you that you can't.

Roman Dad does, of course, have a few of those universal Dad problems – once they're teenagers, the kids can be moody and a bit rude to the slaves, having them put to death for trivial reasons and so on.

Then there are the phases – teenage daughter wanting to join the Vestal Virgins. Roman Dad and Roman Mum are quick to point out what this will mean in terms of orgy invitations. But she won't be told. And the son wants to be a legionnaire and work in Britain. He says the landscape and climate make Tuscany look drab.

It could be worse – at least they don't want to go into politics, or marry each other.

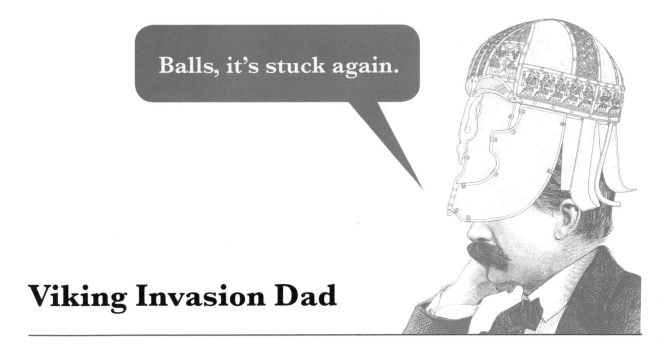

Viking Invasion Dad

If your Dad is a Viking invader, you might have to accept a lot of brothers and sisters with mothers who aren't yours. Though if you're in the real family, back home in Denmark, you probably won't get to meet them.

In fact family life in general is somewhat unorthodox, as Viking Dad is away a lot, sometimes for several years at a stretch. But if and when he returns, you'll get as many solid gold presents as any child could wish for: bangles, hair clips, brooches, necklaces – the classic pillaged booty.

Back at the homestead, Viking Dad's not one to relax. There are plenty of local knockarounds to get stuck into and there's always an axe that needs smithing or a local village that needs plundering.

A good Viking Mum understands Viking Dad's need to let off steam down the meadhall with the boys after a hard day's beserking, but she's always insistent the kids be taught the tools of the trade.

If he's feeling generous, he might let you wear the hat with the upturned horns and see it as his personal duty to show you how to make a man you've just killed into the famous 'blood eagle'.

Battle of Hastings Dad

This Dad gives the young 'uns one heck of a day out.

It's lucky to have a Sir Dad that's so tight with Billy the Conqueror that he's allowed to bring the kids with him.

Once it got started, the battle was a full day's violence

There are not many other children who can say that they took part in the last successful invasion of mainland Britain. There was a bit of waiting for the weather across the Channel, but, once it got started, the battle was a full day's violence.

The army's junior followers were supposed to stay back on the ships, but lots of them found their way to the bottom of the battlefield, from where they could watch the repeated attritional charges and counter-attacks and the steadily accumulating heaps of bodies. It's a fantastic day of learning for all.

When they get home to France, Sir Mum's overjoyed to have them back safe and sound, and she blushes bright red when her son presents her with the head of a slain Englishman. Such a sweet boy.

Father, it's worse than I feared.
I think it could be *Man Flu*.

Black Death Dad

Sometimes it's hard to be a Dad.

When your village, county and country are afflicted with plague is one such time. And it looks as if letting the children keep rats as pets was a bad idea too.

Black Death Dad knows how challenging parenting can be

The whole year and a half that the local population were sprouting buboes, turning black and dropping dead while you talked to them was a tricky time to be a parent.

It certainly wasn't easy after Black Death Mum bought the big one, leaving Black Death Dad as a single parent. Despite his attempts to get back out there, the dating scene's gone a bit quiet of late. Whatever healthy women are left always have a cue of likely lads lining up round the block.

It's not easy grounding your kids for eighteen months. They get stir-crazy. The broken spinning wheel and the key ring with one key on it get boring quickly. Having to lock one out of the house when the boils appear is even harder.

Black Death Dad knows how challenging parenting can be.

You ain't seen me, right?

Machiavellian Dad

Life can be a bit grim if you can't trust your father. And Machiavellian Dad instils this distrust into his children by means of manipulation, betrayal and, in extreme circumstances, torture.

The kids get to have the coolest surname in the class

Much of the time, though, he's great fun, and sees that the family makes the most of court life. After all, those Borgias can be a real laugh sometimes. And the kids get to have the coolest surname in the class.

On the other hand, life isn't all that sweet for Machiavellian Mum. If it's not the endless power lunches with other ambitious couples, then it's Machiavellian Dad's fork-tongued sweet talking that means he's always wangling his way out of the washing-up.

But never forget: in his thinking, this Dad is suspended over a pit of infinite despair and meaninglessness, where fleeting power is the only thing of any worth. Not a good place for a Dad to be.

Shlurrrrrrrrrrp!

Eighteenth-Century Scientist Dad

The kitchen, the front room, the hallway and the downstairs toilet are all filled with bubbling glass flasks and tubes and clamps and burners and more tubes. Eighteenth-Century Scientist Dad is attempting to produce a gas hitherto undiscovered by man.

So when one of them is blown out through the kitchen window and into a nearby wood, it isn't anybody's fault

Eighteenth-Century Scientist Mum has taken most of the twelve children to her mother's so she can write her feminist tract. But two have absconded and are running along the hall throwing vials of acid at each other.

These two children are dearly loved by their father; of this there can be no doubt. But when an experiment is in progress, Dad has to maintain his high state of concentration and cannot be expected to consider all eventualities. So when one of them is blown out through the kitchen window and into a nearby wood, it isn't anybody's fault and nobody thinks any the worse of him.

Things were different then. That's why you had twelve children.

Graham

Graham – With a tendency to laugh at inappropriate moments during films, Graham is a slow-moving, big, round bear of a man who nevertheless enjoys the full range of North Face clothing and always carries a compass or Swiss Army knife. Unable to successfully reverse a car down even the widest street, his greatest fear is driving in the Lake District.

Merde!

Off with his head!

French Revolution Dad

Life with French Revolution Dad starts off as a real blast.

What great 'family time' they've spent hating the aristocracy and watching their beheadings

The kids have begun their lives as grumbling peasants with no hope for any improvement in their existence. So to take part, with Dad, in the storming of the Bastille is an exhilarating experience.

Then there's the sitting round in coffee shops discussing politics with Dad and his cronies and the excitement at the unveiling of the Declaration of the Rights of Man. Meanwhile, French Revolution Mum can't stop telling her story about the march on Versailles. And all that cake to eat as well. Yummy. Will the fun never cease?

And what great 'family time' they've spent hating the aristocracy and watching their beheadings.

But, in the end, the pressure to defame and denounce is irresistible. When the kids eventually turn Dad over to the authorities, the family has finally done its bit in acting as a vague metaphor for the revolution.

Amen

REPENT! THE END OF THE WORLD IS NIGH!

Puritan Dad

For the children of Puritan Dad, there is an upside and a downside.

The upside is that you probably get to go to heaven, if that's your cup of tea. The downside is that for your time here on earth Dad is going to make sure that you behave yourself.

It's not so much the incessant itching or the non-stop preaching, it's the fact that however nice the girlfriend or boyfriend you take home, Puritan Dad isn't going to accept them until there's a ring on their finger. This old man's no easy touch.

His brood are fitted for hair shirts at an early age. Their lives are pretty austere and they can expect to spend quite a bit of time in church and/or reading the Bible. At least they'll never be lost for a pithy proverb.

Puritan Dad's intensity makes him hard to love and live up to, and his fixations with sin and the flesh make him a bit boring. He's certainly not the one to turn to when you need sex education.

His fixations with sin and the flesh make him a bit boring

Rawhide!

Wild West Dad

Wild West Dad falls into two camps – Sheriff Dad and Outlaw Dad.

Sheriff Dad will make sure you can shoot straight and handle yourself in a confrontation with rustlers

Sheriff Dad is a pretty important parent, what with being a Dad *and* upholding the law *and* keeping Outlaw Dad out of town. Sheriff Dad and Outlaw Dad are, of course, mirror images of each other, and their fates are likewise entwined.

Sooner or later they will end up meeting each other in a showdown. All bets are off as to the victor, but if Sheriff Dad has a cleft chin and a macho swagger, he's pretty much a shoo-in.

As parents, both will be aware of the presence of guns around their children.

Outlaw Dad would be more likely to let you take a gun to Outlaw camp and teach you how to mount a horse quickly when leaving a saloon in a hurry, for example. But he's also more likely to shoot at you in a drunken funk.

Sheriff Dad will make sure you can shoot straight and handle yourself in a confrontation with rustlers. And, despite being fancied by the town's best-looking madam, he'll never leave Mum. He's not that type of guy.

I took the mission. What the hell else was I gonna do?

Trench Foot Dad

A postcard arrives home. It is from Trench Foot Dad. It is dated 21st July 1916. The nippers are all excited and want to hear it read again and again.

It's a shame that when he's home on leave all his son wants to know is how many Germans he's killed

It doesn't say much. The most important thing it says is that he is alive. That he has survived the worst single day in the history of the British Army.

The children don't understand why the postcard makes their mother cry, but they remember deeply that it does.

Trench Foot Dad has to fight in some of the worst conditions imaginable, but being away from his wife and children still manages to be additional suffering. It's a shame that when he's home on leave all his son wants to know is how many Germans he's killed.

It doesn't matter though. Children are children.

It's comforting for the man sitting in a building for the first time in three months. What he hopes is that his own children aren't caught up in global conflagration twenty years down the road.

No, it doesn't seem possible.

One small step for Dad... One giant leap for Dadkind...

Space Dad

All the children are jealous of Space Dad's kids. He's so rare. He's like a highly collectable Top Trump, which makes him a tough act to follow.

Space Dad always wants his food in small, freeze-dried packages

He's one of the fittest and most intelligent Dads around, but he's also one of the nerdiest, and tends to have a bad haircut. All that helmet-wearing plays havoc with volume.

Even though she's very proud of her high achiever, Space Mum gets annoyed at meal times because Space Dad always wants his food in small, freeze-dried packages and is very keen that his food be blended.

The trouble with Space Dad is that whatever you are talking about he will eventually say, 'Yes, but up in space things are different.' Plus he's dangerous to drive with because he keeps looking up wistfully.

All the same, it feels good to be with him. This Dad has an aura and makes you feel like you have perspective.

PART
FOUR

The Family Jigsaw

The Family Jigsaw

No Dad is an island. A Dad is one part of a network of family relationships, a cobweb of mutual dependency, a diagram of lines and dots that represent people and the connections between them. Dad sometimes has to switch roles – he's certainly a Dad, but he might also be a son, a brother, even a husband. So, to understand your Dad more deeply, it can help to look at his behaviour towards other relations.

Big Brother

Dads often have brothers and sisters. These brothers and sisters are known as aunts and uncles.

Aunts and uncles are there to buy extravagant birthday and Christmas presents for their nephews and nieces. Often they live abroad or are eccentric or undesirable in some way.

'Uncle Bernard let me fly the aeroplane... Dad, why aren't you an airline pilot?'

The key thing is that they see your Dad not as a Dad, but as their brother.

They bring with them all sorts of metaphorical suitcases and skeleton-enriched wardrobes, a whole history of competition and co-operation, struggle and stand-off, hostility and happiness.

Now, many Dads get on well with their siblings; their shared histories make them feel grounded and connected.

But not all.

There are some things that can make it difficult for Dad to get on with aunts and uncles.

Consider how a Dad must feel if he is strapped to a grinding nine-to-five, mortgaged up to his neck, struggling to make various ends meet various other ends, while

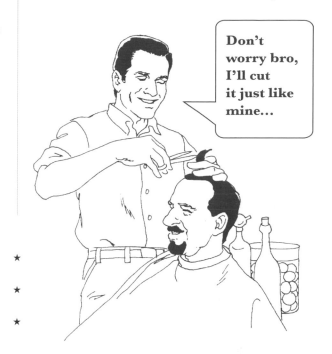

his brother, always the family rebel, a sheep of ultimate darkness, a sheep who moved to London at the age of sixteen, and was the cause of much anxiety and many family rows – a sheep who is now on the TV three nights a week in a prime-time soap opera that Dad despises with all the emotional powers available to him, but which seems to be paying the uncle in question an outrageous amount of money.

Yes, sibling rivalry can certainly affect Dads, especially if they are siblings. The trouble with an annoyingly successful brother or sister is that they can outshine a Dad in all kinds of unpredictable ways.

Dad may love to see his children happy, but he doesn't really want to hear his son, with uncontained excitement, shrieking, 'Dad, Auntie Rosemary took me to the film set and I got to meet Stephen Spielberg and he let me do the clapper-board thing and he gave me a baseball cap and he said if I go back next week I can have a walk-on part as an alien!'

Nor does he want to hear, 'Dad, Uncle Bernard let me fly the aeroplane back from America! Dad, why aren't you an airline pilot?'

Sometimes it's impossible to compete. It may be best just to accept this.

For while it's tempting to try to even things out, to get some sort of revenge, the trouble is that revenge can often backfire on the revenger.

Hearing something like:

'Dad, I told Uncle Bernard that you said he made the family cat run away by tying it to a firework-powered skateboard, and he said that you did that',

Or,

'Dad, Auntie Rosemary says that lots of ladies don't get married and you should mind your own business,' doesn't improve things.

The kids will just end up angry that their aunts and uncles buy them fewer expensive presents than before. Sometimes Dads have no choice but to grit their teeth, smile thinly and say:

'Yes, Uncle Bernard really is a great guy.' The reverse of this problem is when an aunt or uncle is less than successful in life (i.e. deeply unsuccessful).

In some ways it's not such a morale-sapping difficulty for Dad. Uncle Bernard stumbles from low-paid job to low-paid job, turning up at the house every couple of months, smelling of drink and looking to borrow three hundred quid for a sure thing at the 3.15 novice stakes at Kempton.

Auntie Rosemary becomes harder and harder to understand as she skips merrily into her fifth marriage leaving an ever-widening wake of kids and stepkids behind her.

★ Dad certainly doesn't feel outshone, but he may well feel disappointed, tainted, as well
★ as financially taxed.

★ Dad feels the pull of his original family more strongly if someone else is letting the team down.

tick, tick, tick...

'Dad, I told
Uncle Bernard
that you said he
made the family
cat run away
by tying it to a
firework-powered
skateboard, and
he said that you
did that'

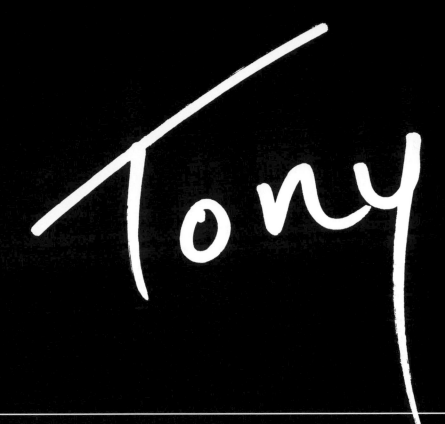

Tony

Tony – Mostly spotted in the South East and Wales and the market towns of Cheshire. A swarthy, rotund man, flamboyant by nature and most likely sporting some variant of facial hair – be it 5 o'clock shadow or for the more mature Tony, a moustache. Tonys like a blazer (single-breasted, double-vented), a belted high trouser or big pocketed Chino (at the weekend), and although ill-advised for the larger man, a penny loafer is Tony's shoe of choice.

In-laws

Even stranger to think about:

Dad has brothers, sisters and parents that aren't his real brothers, sisters and parents (this happens twice if Dad was adopted).

They are known as **in-laws.**

Why can't your sister be more like you?

Even the title sounds something like a threat, like a rule that must never be broken, like a series of commitments as strong as steel chains.

The reason that in-law relationships can be difficult, in fact historically are difficult, is that with blood relations there have usually been many years of mutual discovery and symbiotic accommodation; with in-law relationships this is not the case.

Dad has married the love of his life, the one person about whom he never had a single doubt. The same marriage now links him, in law, to another family, a family he probably doesn't know too well, a family he hardly even noticed when he was love-struck and goofy.

In-laws...even the title sounds like a threat

His new mother is seemingly kind and friendly towards him, but the relationship has an undercurrent of disappointment, disapproval and, more often than not, disbelief.

His new father is usually totally unable to conceal his suspicion. This suspicion will often reveal itself in hostility, verbal sniping and a general tendency to undermine Dad's progress.

Dad's relationships with brothers- and sisters-in-law are unpredictable, ranging from the delightful to the deviant.

The most dangerous outcome of all possible dangerous outcomes is when Dad fancies his sister-in-law.

When this happens, the delicate golden threads that link Dad to his other family become a nightmarish cobweb that drags all sorts of people towards a sort of central vortex of family-related emotional turmoil.

Without being moralistic in any way, it is fair to say that it is immoral for a Dad to act upon his desires for his brother-in-law's keeper.

A Dad needs to uphold his status with his own family. To be found by his own child under the duvet with auntie is a fairly good bet as an event that might destroy a child's respect for his or her Dad.

In-laws are more than just in-laws.

He's Still My Baby

Let's not forget, Dads have Dads.

And Mums.

They are still sons.

Although they spend much of their time, superficially at least, telling others how it should be, Dads themselves still get told what to do too.

Oddly, this is often where they get their wisdom – experience. Dad does know how it feels; he's been there. He's still there. There is someone whose approval or disapproval still matters.

Dad can still be:

☞ A naughty boy, a fool, a child.

Grandma still says stuff like:

☞ 'Don't pick your nose, darling.'

And Grandad still says stuff like:

☞ 'You paid what? Are you deranged?'

Aside from Mum, they are the only people who can say stuff like that to Dad.

★ The student of Dad, ever in search of paternal enlightenment, is interested in how Dad reacts to Grandma and Grandad.

★ Like father like son. Monkey see; monkey do. All that.

★ Is Dad confident in his status as Dad, or does he slide back into an infantile state, which always annoys Mum to the point where she chews her hair and calls Dad by his actual name?

Becoming a Dad should, perhaps and possibly, be a significant point of release, a letting-go, not only adopting a new role, but shedding an old one.

But that's all easily said. If Dad still shows his bank statements and bills to his Dad, he may not have cut the eminently cutable ties that bind. The same goes for passing on to Mum the domestic commentary of his Mum – observations about tidiness, femininity, maternal qualities.

Mister Lover Man

Before Dad gets to be a Dad, he is a lover.

It can be that Dad is a lover only once, but most Dads slide into domesticity all too quickly. They get married or live in sin.

So it's likely that Dad has had a previous life, a pre-Dad persona, a romancing-Mum persona. This kind of thing is notoriously difficult for offspring to think about.

Parents are parents: bland characters who ask about school and tell you when you can leave the table. They are not hot-blooded, bed-sheet-ruffling, animalistic cavorters.

Oh, but they are. Or they certainly were, and, knowing Dad, something is still going on.

PART
FIVE

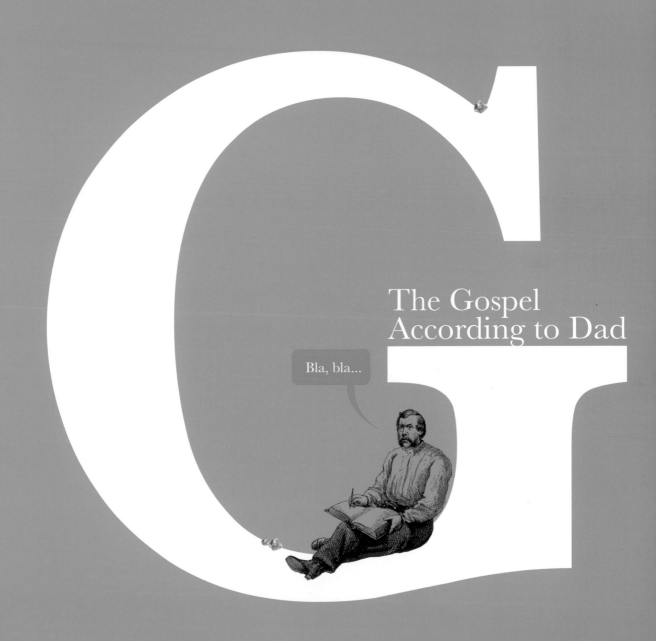

It's all
about
the kids

The Gospel
According to Dad

The experienced Dad has much to teach the newcomer. All that experience, for one thing. The terrors and the tears, from infancy to adulthood. Those badges of honour – chicken pox, swimming clubs, broken limbs, parents' evenings. When children go through phases, so do parents – phases of reaction to their children's phases – and they pay an emotional price. The price, however, can be reduced. Knowing how to be a good Dad requires a complex toolkit. Fear not, though. That knowledge can be communicated in writing. Here, bringing all the bacon back home, Dad tells it like it is.

The Credo

I am a Dad. It's how I see myself; it's who I am. I live it; I breathe it; I love it. And I pride myself on how seriously I take my role. If someone comes up to me in the street and asks me what it's all about, I've got absolutely no doubt about my answer – it's all about the kids. That's what it's all about. The kids. My kids. And I dedicate myself to bringing them up right.

Amen

creeeeek!

Walking & Talking

Kids become more interesting when they get properly mobile and start nattering.

But once they start shuffling and staggering about and asking all sorts of mad questions, your life gets even busier.

What should you do with these babbling bundles of fun?

The answer: you have to interact with them.

Keep a close eye on the kids when they're learning to walk, because they like to launch themselves, face-first, towards just about any type of pointed sharp thing.

You have to watch the toddling for as long as they do that Frankenstein's monster walk. Let them hold your hand when they are getting started.

Or, if you don't fancy vacating the armchair every five minutes, set up a series of cables at about eighteen inches above the floor, so the little tykes have something to hold on to in the early upright stages.

The main thing about children and speech development is swearing.

You have to retrain yourself first of all. A good method is to imagine that your gran is always with you.

You probably won't want to do too much cussing in front of her, so you won't do it in front of the youngsters.

You really do have to try to cut it out, because they will pick it up before you can say '********ing m**********er.'

I always think there's nothing worse than a two-year-old yapping profanities at pensioners in a shopping centre.

Always remember to stop imagining that gran is with you when the babbler goes to bed.

If you don't, things get sort of odd.

********ing
m**********er.

gran

Pets

Pets become desirable to children from about the age of five.

Pets bring out the best and the worst in them:

The best in that they want to love and care for something.

The worst in that they want to love and care for something without actually making the effort to clean, feed, water, exercise, etc.

Although letting your children keep pets can be a chore, it's an effective way of teaching them a number of life's lessons. Chores and responsibility, for starters.

And pets teach kids other important facts too, facts about procreation and death in particular.

They act as prompts for Q&A sessions. So be ready suddenly to hear:

'Daddy, Cuthbert and Catherine are playing piggy-back!'

Or,

'Reginald's fallen asleep and gone all stiff!'

You can use these spontaneous conversations to inform the kids about the birds and the bees without involving Mummy and Daddy and the attendant unpleasant imagery this brings.

Be in no doubt, you need delicacy and subtlety in order to get it right. You will have to judge what sort of information can be managed by the emotional maturity of your child.

'That's just the way guinea pigs hug when they love each other,' might be enough for one child.

Another might need to know that, 'Well, Catherine is in oestrus and Cuthbert can sense this, is aroused and so attempts to mate with her. The growling is just a noise Daddies, I mean guinea pigs, make when they're happy in a particular way.'

So, pets can be good things for the development of your whippersnapper, but it does all depend on the age of the kids and your own home circumstances.

A Dad is *not* just for Christmas...

It may be fashionable for those living on sink estates to keep a pit-bull in the bathroom or an Asian python in the airing cupboard, but my advice is not to go leaping into anything drastic.

Start small.

Hamsters and mice don't take too much looking after and do introduce little ones to the painful fact that something small, cute and fluffy can bite your fingernail off if you are not careful.

A couple of tiny rodents in a cage should allow you to gauge whether or not little Emily is ready for the responsibility.

If she's not, they don't live too long.

Rabbits and guinea pigs are the next step up. They take a bit more looking after (they live longer too) and draw a bit more blood when they bite.

Of course cats and dogs are top of the tree as they interact in a meaningful way with people, and this is what all the years of children's fiction have taught kids to expect from anything with fur.

Cats don't take too much looking after, but all the interaction has to be on their terms.

Dogs have that loyalty and enthusiasm thing going for them, but they need walking a lot, and that will fall to you, because most kids cannot commit to anything other than themselves for the kind of period of time a dog might be expected to live.

That's just the way guinea pigs hug when they love each other

Ray – A close, yet poorer relation of Tony. He sells books, but would give it all up tomorrow to go back to selling cars. Due to a thirty-year diet of Light and Bitter ('you get one and a half pints for the price of one') and fried foods, Ray is impotent. Never out of his one suit, even on the beach, as far as Ray is concerned fashion is the preserve of 'queers and lebanons'.

PART SIX

P

The
Psychology
of Dad

The Psychology of Dad

Hold on to your homburg, here comes the psychology. When it comes to the study of Dad, enlightening stuff with which to enlighten us. Theories, complexes, repressions, sublimations – who'd have thought being a Dad was so complicated, so fraught? Well, in one sense it isn't. That's right. The great thing about psychology is that you don't have to know anything. Or even do anything. Just do what comes 'naturally' and you're there.

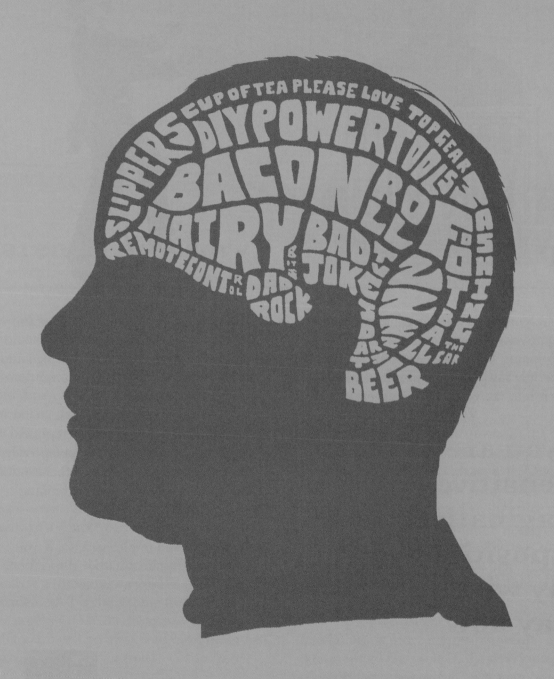

Robin — Usually married to Fiona and most often found with three teenage kids (Zak, Solomon and Daisy), Robin is fervently anti-nuclear, a keen recycler and enjoys the excellent driving position of his brand-new S-Class Mercedes. An architect by trade, and stupendously rich, Robin has always struggled with the private/state school dilemma.

PART
SEVEN

The Natural Dad

The Natural Dad

Psychology is all very well. But psychological enquiry raises the study of Dad to an other-worldly level of great complexity. For many people this can cause headaches and temporary blindness. There are other ways of studying the paternal existence. A nice, straightforward method of enquiry is to look at the way that other members of the animal kingdom, animal Dads that is, go about their everyday fatherly business.

Yo, Dad turn the heating down!

Dad Endures

For Dad stamina no one can compete with the emperor penguin.

But Emperor Penguin Dad has no choice. In true Dad style, he just gets on with it

After mating season, female emperor penguins produce a single egg. Once they've done this, they pass the egg to Emperor Penguin Dad, who has to look after it and keep it, and himself, alive through the Antarctic winter, while Emperor Penguin Mum goes back to sea for several months to fill up on fish and squid and hang out with the girls. The nerve.

While child care for human Dads usually means dropping the youngster off somewhere on the way to work, all the Emperor Penguin Dads huddle together in the bleak and freezing wilderness and play their parts in forming a giant snowy crèche.

The slowly rotating crèche is a great example of the power of Dads in Nature. While this can't be described as a 'hands-on' kind of fatherhood – the penguins have no hands – it certainly requires a level of commitment that many human Dads would baulk at.

But Emperor Penguin Dad has no choice. In true Dad style, he just gets on with it. He keeps his egg warm in a brood pouch, which doesn't sound very Dad, but nevertheless is a serious macho business in the worldview of the penguin. More macho, say, than a man bag.

Gary

Gary – The youngest child of three, a suspicious seven years after number two, Gary has found solace in a wardrobe full of matching tracksuits and his better than average football skills.

I like pussy

His Majesty

Mirror mirror etc. – who is the macho-est natural Dad of all?

What you really want if you are a wild animal Dad is not just to be seen as the patriarch of your family. What you want is to be acknowledged as the supreme something, the pinnacle of a whole environment.

Cue the king of the jungle: Lion Dad.

The male lion even has a special hairdo to make him stand out and seem even more regal. His mane is an indicator of his virility – big mane equals much macho potency and potential.

That may be comparable to human appearance and explain why bald men are seen as less sexually desirable. However, these hairless wonders make up for it by being high-earning investment bankers, accountants, Soviet leaders and suchlike – employing optional mate-attracting strategy not available to lions.

Not only does lordly Leo slack about most of his time, he leaves the gazelle, wildebeest, and antelope hunting to Mrs Lion

There are more connections to be made. For eighty per cent of the day Lion Dad does nothing, preferring to lounge around and sleep in the shade. Sound familiar?

Not only does lordly Leo slack about most of his time, he leaves the gazelle, wildebeest, and antelope hunting to Mrs Lion, just like Mrs Dad hunting for 2-for-1s, Club Card points earners and home-brand products in Tesco during the weekly grocery shop.

But, Lion Dad, regal and awesome though he is, is still as much a victim of merciless Nature as he is an example of it. His opportunity for leading and being able to defend his own pride is brief, probably a couple of years at the most.

The pressure on the king of the jungle can lead to some truly shocking behaviour. When a male takes over a pride, he will need to kill any cubs fathered by his predecessor, in order that the new Mrs Lions become receptive to his charms. It's simple and it's brutal. And it is in no way like the Dads that we know or may be.

Killing stepchildren is wrong. The lion, remember, is king of the jungle. And people have spent centuries trying to civilise the jungle out of human life. He's handsome, he's powerful, he's emblematic: But he's not like us.

If there's any justice in the world...

The King of the Swingers

The Darwinian take on evolution would suggest that the paternal practices of gorillas, orang-utans and chimpanzees can shed some light on the unlit parts of Dad. Knowing where you've come from to know where you're going, etc.

Surely the great apes, with their knowing expressions, apparent laughter and complex social lives, are more instructive when we think of our own behaviour and motivation.

Well, you might think that. But, you know, Nature doesn't adhere to Disney's rules. Sure, chimps can ride bicycles and smoke cigarettes, but, according to films and so on, they can wield clubs and grimace menacingly too. So, don't expect it to be all good news from the front lines of simian similarity simulation.

As every schoolboy knows, primates range from humans – at the top needless to say – all the way down to lemurs. So what does Lemur Dad have to tell us about the Art of Dad in general? Well, surprise surprise, Lemur Dad lives under the thumb.

Lemurs live in small social groups where the top lemur is a female. So he has an immediate connection with his homo sapiens cousins there. Ouch.

Like all primates, Lemur Dad needs to work his way up if he is to become the dominant Dad. And he has to compete for Lemur Mum. The competition for Lemur Mum involves rubbing your scent on your tail and waving it about in front her face: the primate equivalent of wearing a Ralph Lauren shirt and Hugo Boss aftershave – just as offensive and just as likely to work.

Gorilla Dad

People are not lemurs. That much seems clear. Then perhaps they are more like gorillas. Gorillas have had a century of bad press thanks to King Kong and all that. We know now that gorillas are not the monstrous, sky-scraper-climbing nutters we once thought. They are mild-mannered vegetarians and highly tolerant of documentary makers.

This great power gives him ultimate responsibility

In fact Gorilla Dad is, it turns out, one of Nature's top Dads. The reason? It's his combination of awesome power and gentleness towards the young that make him such a great example.

Just like Human Dad (in some cases) he has the most physical power and experience in the troop. This great power gives him ultimate responsibility. If there are problems – the gorilla equivalent of a cracked water pipe, a leaky faucet, a flat battery – the family look to Gorilla Dad to fix it.

He decides when the group moves on, he arbitrates in family disputes, he disciplines the youngsters. He gives a mean hug. He's just like your Dad or just like you. He might even look like your Dad. Or like you.

Three Happy Meals, and a Big Mac Meal please...

Orang Dad

Similarly, your Dad might look like an orang-utan. Orang-utans are different to gorillas, but still pretty much like people. Or, at least, they aspire to be people. Just listen to King Louie in the Jungle Book.

They aspire to be people. Just listen to King Louie in the Jungle Book.

Orang Dad is one of the cleverest Dads in the wild – a fact his palm leaf rain hats and rhythmic singing and dancing can attest to – but his fathering skills leave something to be desired.

He's like a divorced Dad. He's the kind of guy who likes to roam around, doesn't live at home, a Dad who likes his own space. Wherever he lays his banana, etc. His kids just aren't a big part of his life.

Seems a bit lonely as an example for a human Dad though. Those single men in McDonald's with their kids on a Sunday afternoon – are they our orangs?

I'm a natural.

Chimp Dad

Can chimps out-Dad gorillas? Well, chimpanzee society is rough around the edges.

In terms of family, chimps live a soap opera sort of life – long-term relationships peppered with brief liaisons and bastard children, rows and fights, dominant males and scheming subordinates.

It's not easy being a Chimp Dad, having to put up with all the bickering and never getting any time away from the brood. If ever there was a Dad who understood the ups and downs of 'quality family time', this is him.

If it all sounds too familiar, consider too that Chimp Dad, subject like us to an existence fuelled by power and desire, loves his kids.

That's why we look to simian Dads: they raise their offspring, they teach them about the forest, keep them tidy, tickle them for fun. These guys know what it's all about. Chimp Dads are natural Dads.

If ever there was a Dad who understood the ups and downs of 'quality family time'...

PART EIGHT

T

The
Dad-
to-Be...

The Dad-to-Be

If being a Dad is incredibly easy, becoming one is incredibly simple. It is, of course, life-changing. It's life-making too. You wander and wonder around for years, not being able to figure out what life might mean or even if it means anything at all, and then suddenly you're making some of it for yourself. The terminology is easy – you're going to be someone's Dad. A role not for the faint of heart; a role for a Champion.

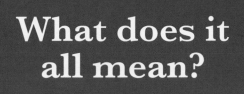

REMEMBER, REMAIN CALM...

embrace the panic...panic is your friend...

Before

Avoiding Panic

You are out in the garden, puffing away on the pipe, sorting out the new shelves for the shed, when your lover comes a-skittering down the garden path, tear-stained face, used pregnancy indicator strip in one hand, sherry in the other.

Panic needs to be ignored. Panic is not what anyone wants from a Dad

'Darling,' she says, 'I'm going to have a baby.'

Obviously, your first reactions are likely to be ones of unbounded joy. You might join your wife in having a sherry, early though it is. You might delay the shelving and stand talking excitedly in the kitchen about what will need to be done to convert the spare room into a nursery. And after supper and another sherry and another go with the ready-rubbed, you feel a warm glow of achievement. Your biology works. You're going to be … a Dad. Welcome to the gang, kid.

But as you settle back in your armchair, slip off your brogues and put up your feet, you sense a slight discomfort, a lowly voice out of harmony with the glorious chorus of triumph that is the new you. And the lowly voice seems to be getting louder.

This is panic. Panic says things like:

- ☛ *But what if something goes wrong with the pregnancy?*

- ☛ *And what if when they do the scan they find something wrong?*

- ☛ *We can't afford a baby right now. Where's the money going to come from?*

- ☛ *Am I old or mature enough to be a Dad? I'm only forty-five.*

Panic needs to be ignored. Panic is not what anyone wants from a Dad. The Dad-to-Be quickly finds sources of panic he didn't know were available. He has to be able to silence them or keep them bearable. He has to live with them.

> Oh, you are so cute...

> Yes, *now* I am cute, but soon you will grow to hate me.

Living with a Beach Ball

Long before any child appears, connubial life begins to change.

For the imminent Dad that may involve imminent Mum being sick a lot, not being able to tolerate various smells, choosing some interesting meals and so forth.

Pretty soon a little bump appears. And at first it's cute. Along with the grainy ultrasound picture, it is proof of your great achievement. Something is growing, and it's down to you. Half of it is at least. You may find yourself giving the foetus a nickname, say *Tiny* or *Weeny* or *Little Tadpole of the Rising Moon*, for example. It will soon outgrow this.

The last couple of months before Day Zero, when the nursery is painted and the little blankets and sleep suits are safely stowed in the new IKEA drawers, are like living with a woman with a beach ball up her jumper.

And the wind of change will certainly blow through the windmills of your mind when you realise that the woman who once looked so irresistible in that black skirt and those heels just shuffled and waddled past in carpet slippers and a sagging track suit, sneezing and blowing her nose as though it's some new form of communication.

But, New Man that you are, you can share the experience of beach-ball birthing if you must. The ante-natal classes are for couples. Be aware though that this is not the meeting where you get up, recite your name and admit to being alcoholic.

The early classes teach you how to breathe and how to relax. Neither of these skills is usually too taxing for the average Dad-in-waiting. One problem is that the classes are often weekday evenings. After a full day at work and a rushed meal, it is not unusual once a fifteen-minute relaxation session is over to find three or four prospective Dads asleep in their chairs. Heroes, all.

It isn't all sitting around breathing. You get to practise rolling a tennis ball on your partner's back; you get to zap yourself with a TENS machine; you get to watch a video of a woman giving birth in a great big paddling pool. You can still hear the screams months after.

Two tips:

If invited to draw a shape with a marker on A4 paper, bear in mind that you may be asked to move your pelvis in this shape later in the session. The man who draws a dodecahedron is headed for injury.

And do not volunteer for anything. Before you know it you'll be linking arms with other exhausted-looking oafs and miming the contractions of a uterus wall, as you drive a large blue cushion down into a birth canal dramatically improvised by a computer programmer called Matt and a pet shop manager called Dustin.

It's a grim and sober kind of hokey-cokey that ends when the woman claps her hands and shouts gleefully, 'Okay, guys, you were excellent. Weren't they, ladies?' Good preparation only for the humiliations fatherhood brings.

Inhale, exhale, inhale, exhale, inhale, exhale, inhale, exhale, inhale, exhale, inhale, exhale, come on man, *breath*!

Saying Goodbye to Yourself

Prospective Dads, especially those happy to be so, often fail to realise one of the most dramatic aspects of initial fatherhood. Whoever you are or think you are, you no longer will be. Put simply – those days are gone.

Even if someone tells you this you still don't believe it. Okay, having a child will be a bit more restricting, there'll be some sleepless nights and difficult days, but it can't change you as a person, can it? You are who you are and all that.

Wrong, so very wrong.

What prospective Dads ignore is that you are bound to be different; there will be more of you. Yes, more of you. Because the new arrival will be part of you.

If you are what you think and do, and you might be, then it's goodbye to the old you

The prospective Mum has known it for a while, but Dad will only get it once the bawling bambino is in his hands. If you are what you think and do, and you might be, then it's goodbye to the old you.

You will find yourself thinking things like, 'Support the baby's head!' and 'The nappy

needs changing again?' a lot more than 'I think I'll have another beer' or 'Another hour in bed sounds beautiful'. But all that is mere surface nonsense. The fundamental change is philosophical, existential, even spiritual.

Because you become, paradoxically enough, more and less mortal. You are less mortal because there is a part of you that is something new, outliving you. You feel more mortal because someone has to look after this impossibly fragile life and that someone is you. Your life, as they say, is no longer your own.

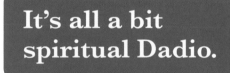

It's all a bit spiritual Dadio.

Money and Worry

You may be born into a family of billionaires, inheriting vast wealth and the structures to keep generating such riches, living a life of opulence and excess and never having to work a day in your life. In which case, any time is fine for having a baby.

For everyone else, there is, as the limerick says, never a right time. The average cost of raising a child is about the price of buying a house. So don't expect your bank account not to notice when a child is born.

Obviously a sensible Dad will cut his cloth to suit his cloth availability. Having a Savile Row tailor knocking up the little ones' romper suits is an option, but not a sensible one for most.

At this point many Dads-to-Be will undergo a phenomenon known as squirrelling. Squirrelling is putting stuff by for leaner times and in this case should include money, alcohol, cigarettes and chocolate, power tools, auto accessories, anything like that. As with life during wartime, all will become increasingly valuable in the post-birth world.

In another way, these aren't financial sacrifices, they are investments. You are investing in the future of your child. After all, someone invested in you.

See you in Barbados!

During

Avoiding Panic

There are a number of easy ways to eliminate the need for minor panics once labour begins. You should already have the hospital bag packed. Make sure there's petrol in the car. Your wife will take several years to see the funny side if she has to deliver at a BP twenty-four-hour garage because you had to stop for fuel and a bag of crisps.

A long labour means being stuck at home for hours waiting for some sort of progress

The main source of potential panic early in labour is that the baby will arrive before you get to the delivery room – in the hallway, in the back of the car, at the BP twenty-four-hour. It all runs through the about-to-be-Dad's mind.

And, unless the labour is pretty quick, you can't just whiz down to the hospital. They'll send you back. It's like trying to get in a trendy nightclub – if your contractions aren't good enough you're not getting in.

A long labour means being stuck at home for hours waiting for some sort of progress. This waiting can give you time to worry. It's best to do something purposeful, like eating a meal, calling close relatives to keep them in touch, checking the car has petrol.

Julian – One of those rare breeds of men who have wide hips, double-jointed elbows and cannot catch. A lecturer in film studies at Oxford Poly and married to a natural birth councillor who is proud to have breastfed their only child up to and slightly beyond its third birthday. Julian couldn't be happier.

Being Useful

Once the process has really got going and you're there in the delivery room it can be intense for Dads. It's pretty intense for Mums too, don't forget.

Your principal role may be going to get a cup of tea, or asking for one of those cardboard bowls you puke into

All that husband stuff you happily signed up for at the wedding is really starting to come back to haunt you. Seeing your loved one in pain and being able to do nothing to help but read a newspaper is difficult.

You will want to be useful and supportive; you're certainly getting the easier of the two available rides here and you should bear all that in mind. No need to rush in and start rubbing a tennis ball against anyone's back. Your wife will tell you what she wants you to do.

The midwives often leave you to your own devices, assuming you'll scream or something if you need them, so your principal role may be going to get a cup of tea, or asking for one of those cardboard bowls you puke into, or going back to the car to have another look for the birdsong-and-country-gardens CD.

The Myth of Being Useful

Childbirth is something women do.

There comes a point where the tennis ball, the gas and air, the dextrose tablets all become irrelevant and there's nothing else to fetch (except the camera), and the role of imminent Dad is largely not to annoy imminent Mum.

This can vary. Some birth-givers will not even notice the father-to-be at the periphery of the natal experience; others may want someone to count and breathe along with them.

You might feel a little stupid sitting there saying, 'And breathe and push. And breathe and push. Come on and push now. Come on. You can push better than that! Push! Hold it! Breathe and breathe and push! And push! You've got to push more! Come on! Keep pushing!' but it's not much of a sacrifice compared to intense bodily trauma.

Think what would have been different without you there. Not much, probably. For centuries, and in many cultures still, Dads did not attend the birth. Don't get it into your head that you're needed.

Come on, love, work with me! Yeah, Baby!

Service

One aspect of the miracle of birth that really does bring a smile to tight and worried lips is the hospital staff. They do their utmost to introduce a kind of crazy sitcom magic to the whole thing.

They do their utmost to introduce a kind of crazy sitcom magic to the whole thing

They have lots of madcap gags to keep you laughing and stop you worrying. Look out for the bed that won't tilt then keeps collapsing, the consultant who keeps calling you by someone else's name, the midwife who comes in, turns on a radio tuned to an in-your-face pirate station and then leaves. It's so good they must rehearse this stuff.

Watch out for the baby's vital signs machine; this goes on and off to see if you're paying attention. Watch out too for the midwife smiling broadly and asking if you've been shown the tea and coffee facilities while she presses a big red button marked *Emergency*.

In the end, though, they do help you to get your baby safely into the world, and that's the only performance you have to judge. Three cheers!

Blood

Let's not forget that there's a nitty-gritty angle to birth. The angle that fathers-to-be's forefathers didn't have to witness.

Modern Dad's insistence on being there, for whatever reasons, means that he will probably get to see some blood. A surprising amount of blood.

It suddenly seems to be everywhere – on the sheets, the floor, the doctor – and can make you feel a bit rough. Fortunately, unless the whole process really has got out of hand, it's not your blood. Unfortunately it is the blood of your loved one.

You are now at the furthest point from catalogue photographs of impossibly cute infants in gorgeous powder-blue sleep suits and matching night caps that it's possible to get. The blood is the *Alien* moment, the wild animal moment. It's Dads' language.

PART NINE

How To

Be a Dad

How To Be a Dad

Dads have means and methods. There are Dad ways to do things which should come naturally to the family patriarch. They should fit like comfy slippers, or that old Christmas jumper that's okay for gardening. There can sometimes be a bit of chafing, but a strong, upright Dad doesn't admit defeat. Anyway, it's not like it's a job you can resign from. You keep trying till either you get it right, Mum tells you to stop, or you die. If the first of these possibilities sounds the most desirable, heeding advice can help.

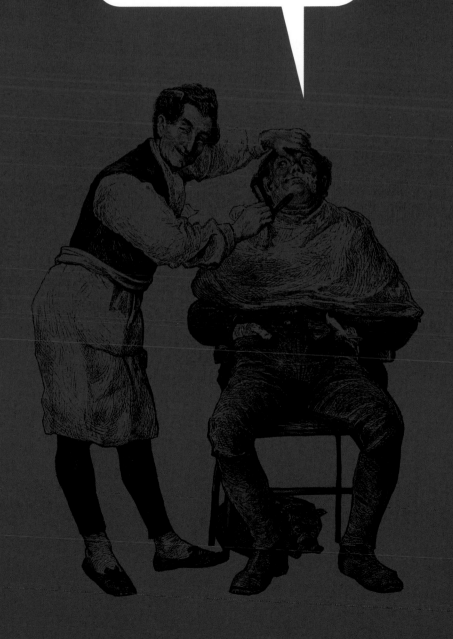

How to Wash the Car

There are three basic Dad approaches to getting the jalopy shined up again. The easiest car-washing regime is never to wash it. It's a nice, simple idea, but forget it. Even if your car is a black 4x4 that looks as though it's supposed to be dirty, Mum will never buy it.

Even if your car is a black 4x4 that looks as though it's supposed to be dirty, Mum will never buy it

The opposite end of the automobile-cleansing timetable schedule is to wash the car diligently every Sunday morning. This is the approach favoured by conscientious and organised Dads. It sets a good example and is a practice that the kids can join in with so they can feel that they are helping Dad, being grown-up, etc.

Washing the car every Sunday goes along with keeping an accurate and complete service history and all receipts for spending on the car during its lifetime.

There is, though, a compromise, in-between, neither-one-thing-nor-t'other approach. This is to put the darned thing through the carwash every couple of months, and just before in-law visits, MOTs, anything where the impression of a conscientious and organised Dad is required. Like all Dad-associated tasks, it's about finding your own rhythm.

Papa's got a brand new Flymo!

How to Mow the Lawn

If you think mowing the lawn is a straightforward Dad task, prepare to be disabused of your simplistic notion. There are certain basics – you need a lawn, a lawn mower and a non-rain-soaked day. But there is no escaping the fact that mowing the lawn is an important task in a number of ways.

It is a way for Dad to survey the outside of his property, be it a Surrey mansion with eight hectares, a paddock and a beech wood, or a two-bedroom terrace with a scabby 12'x15' patch of grass out the back.

As all Dads know, a lawn mower is a frank and forthright means of expressing patriarchal status. Dad A might opt for one of those leather-bucket-seat, high-performance, fuel-injected dragsters; Dad B might only feel the need or the economic ability for a self-assemble, papier-mâché, disposable lawn-chewing system. Shears or a scythe are not tools of the Twenty-First-Century Dad.

The mowing methods available to Dad are stripes or roundels. The first requires cutting parallel lines, the second, concentric circles. Stripes are easier. And it tends to be more fancy Dads who go for the roundels.

It is, if your garden is big enough, possible to draw pictures or even write words across your lawn with the mower. The lawn can be a tempting canvas for the expressive Dad. Remember, if you fear the wrath of Mum, you can always mow over any such artistry when you are finished.

Do be careful though – faint traces may remain afterwards. You don't want *In-Laws Go Home* faintly visible in three-foot letters in front of the house throughout the summer.

Right, got my tools, now how do I get out of the bloody car park...

How to DIY

DIY. Yes, hip, hip, hooray for DIY. Or DDD – Definitive, Dad, Domain.

DIY is the heart of Dad Land

DIY is the heart of Dad Land. That landscape of ladders and lino, pale dust sheets and paint pots, in which a tooled-up Dad battles the forces of drabness, decay and dilapidation.

The wonderful thing about DIY is that it has so many levels on which a Dad can perform his own homeowner heroics. But enough with the alliteration already. Where does all this come from?

Dad's DIY thing owes something to both humanity's hunter-gatherer, cave-dwelling past, as well as the recent predominance of DIY superstores and home makeover TV shows.

Dad has an instinctive urge to retile the bathroom, fix the guttering and gut the kitchen. It is, in the real world, the case that Mum may need to remind Dad of these instincts. Spurred to action, few Dads can resist the satisfaction of a home improvement task successfully completed.

Not only is DIY comparable with the feminine decorative urge, it overlaps. From the original nursery design in the early years, to the new kitchen and bathroom in married maturity, Mum is Dad's compass, his architect, designer, furnishings selector, guru. Dad's DIY is often Mum's dream.

But all this is to detract from what is essential Dad territory. Mum may weigh in with advisory asides, but most of the time DIY is quality Dad time. Alone.

Focused on practicalities – the size of the rawlplug, the bubble in the spirit level – Dad stands to experience a real sense of purpose. He is improving his home, smoothing rough edges, giving what he can to his family. He is being pure Dad.

In this sense, the great thing about DIY is that it's inclusive. The Dad who retiles the roof of his bungalow and changes the washer on the dripping bath tap is up there, making the world a better place.

He can wipe his forehead with his sleeve, sigh emphatically, put the tools away, and, sweating confidently, smile reassuringly at Mum and say something like *Let's have a cup of tea, shall we?* safe in the knowledge that she will show her appreciation in her own special way later.

Changing a fuse is nowhere nearly as erotic as re-turfing the back lawn

Obviously this kind of Dad reward is not going to be the same regardless of the task performed. Changing a fuse is nowhere nearly as erotic as re-turfing the back lawn or installing a decoratively tiled en suite.

Damn! It hurts to look this good!

How to Wear a Suit and Tie

Dads are just little boys who have grown up and had families.

Dad, if he gets a moment, can still remember the telling off he got when, aged eleven, he came home caked in mud from BMXing through the woods with his mates after a week of intense rain.

He knows all there is to know about wrapping a narrow piece of cloth round his neck and fixing it in a sliding knot

It never occurred to him that clothes didn't magically clean, condition and iron themselves before tucking themselves neatly away in his drawers. Similarly, he couldn't understand his mother's apoplexy when he came home, aged thirteen, having ripped holes in both knees of his trousers and both elbows of his sweater while out skateboarding with his pals. Why did you have to be smart?

But riding along beside this ragamuffin's adventures was an awareness of life's formality: the school uniform (no grass stains on the knees!), the crazy suit bought for him when he was a pageboy at his uncle's wedding (his first experience of velvet), the jacket only ever worn for visiting grandparents.

Some Dads like and feel comfortable with the smart look, many do not.

Let's go New Raving.

Many Dads shame their kids with their eccentric informality – the golf jumper over the green overalls, the oversized jeans from a charity shop. There are also many who know that the school ethic – ironed shirt, top button fastened, tie tight – carries on into grown-up life.

Over the years Dad has tied numerous ties thousands of times. He knows all there is to know about wrapping a narrow piece of cloth round his neck and fixing it in a sliding knot. He knows that there are three options:

☞ Regular

☞ Thin

☞ Fat.

He also knows that ties are subject to something called fashion. Serious Dads stick with the regular, whatever fashion might try and dictate. Job interviews, important meetings, a fat or a thin will send the wrong message.

Dad's best tie look is when he's reclined on the sofa, beer in hand, top button undone and a purple silk regular knot loose on his chest. This is what fashion might call 'Raw Dad'.

Chris

Chris – Lovely sandy-haired Chris is kind
to animals, gives generously to charity, but
unfortunately suffers from dry skin on the elbows.
Tall and lean and not unattractive, Chris has an
annoying habit of reading other people's papers
on the tube and apologising for things that aren't
really his fault. Curiously, Chris was one of the
first men in Britain to drink Coke Zero.

Come on kids! Lets P.A.R.T.Y!

Spike, tell me that's not your Old Man?

How to Have a Party

Pre-teens

Everyone likes a party. Children included. Eventually they will get the idea that they could host their own. Clever little blighters.

There are different kinds of children's parties depending most on how old the child is. From four or five years old to nine or ten, children want one kind of party. From thirteen or fourteen onwards, they have a different kind of shindig in mind. As far as Dad is concerned, both kinds have nightmarish potential.

Dads, and particularly Mums, can get a little competitive when it comes to party time for the young 'uns. Your child's party certainly can't be any less spectacular than the ones he or she has been to, where gifts were lavish and a bouncy castle was only the half of it.

Dad has to venture into the jaw-bitingly expensive world of clowns and magicians, called Bongo or Marvo, and people who tell stories about animals with stupid names and make hats and bicycles out of balloons.

The day itself must, by its very nature – a dozen or more sugared-up five-year-olds running amok, hitting each other, being sick, failing to use the toilet correctly – tend towards the chaotic, and has to be endured.

Dad gets to be thankful that he's not Mum, as he watches her making the jellies and the cake. His job is merely to light the candles and make sure no hyperactive guests suffer burns. And that's a pointer to what your basic aims are – the children, especially yours, have a good time, nothing gets broken and no one gets hurt.

Teens

The basic aims are the same for the teenager party, only the stakes are higher. It is a good idea, if possible, to find a venue that isn't your house. If there is no alternative to having it at home, there are rules and precautions to think about.

It's not necessarily about trusting your own kids. People gatecrash parties, particularly teenagers. Dad knows this; he did it himself. So, assuming and planning for the worst is advisable.

Dad may decide that he needs to be in his house, guarding the castle as it were, from beginning to end, or he may give in to sustained moaning and agree to take Mum out somewhere for the evening. If he stays, he is in for a hard night of repelling the uninvited, monitoring the drinking and smoking of everyone he sees, and repeatedly discouraging teenage couples from disappearing into bedrooms.

Going out is easier, but takes a little more nerve and a little more preparation. How much work would it be to move all the furniture into one, lockable bedroom and to take up the carpets and store them in the garage? Quite a lot.

It may seem like a drastic measure, but the alternative is a future of constantly noticing the dark circle on the living-room carpet where a young lady was once sick, occasionally feeling sad that the carriage clock no longer works, and frequently remembering that the reveller who poured enough of Dad's single malt into the fish tank to kill even the snails remains at large.

Even the best party has to stop some time. Have this agreed with your kids in advance. It can't be too early, or they'll feel hard done by. Err on the side of caution; no coming home in time for your regular bedtime.

Once the cinema, the restaurant and the drink in a local bar are all done, and it's still not the agreed time, you may find yourself with nowhere to go. The most common Dad response is to park up by the forecourt of a petrol station and eat crisps and drink some carbonated syrup while listening to Radio 5 Live. Mum may well be asleep already by this time.

If you are lucky, when you get home your house will be a mess, but one that can be fixed without too much financial and/or emotional expense.

There must be over three hundred people here!

God Bless Myspace!

Who said anything about the kids!

How to Do Sports Day

The weather has turned out nice again, the school year is coming to an end, and the children are in a high state of excitement. Sports Day has it all – Pure Dad Country. And, double bonus, neither Mum nor Dad has to do any organising whatsoever.

There is, of course, one thing – competition. Not only are you watching your own kids, trying their little hearts out and panting their way excitedly to those triumphant or abysmal childhood emotional extremes, but you are watching them compete with other children whose parents are also watching. And then the parents get their go. Yes, there's a morsel of edginess at Sports Day.

Competition is a funny thing. Dad knows it exists. He sees it every day. The world can be a tough, competitive place. Protecting his children from, and introducing them to the harsh ways of the world is a long balancing act for Dad.

And then the parents get their go. Yes, there's a morsel of edginess at Sports Day

On Sports Day he will need both his stories ready. Dad can whoop it up with the kids if they triumph and praise to his heart's content. Or, Dad can commiserate and sympathise: *It's not the winning, it's the taking part.* All that stuff is useful and vaguely true.

All of this is subject to one all-important factor: how sporty is Dad? Sportiness is often inherited – just ask racehorse breeders – and for some Dads Sports Day is an opportunity to relive youthful conquest and glory. Occasionally you pity their children, but more often than not they get their laurel wreaths, as if genetically bequeathed.

If Dad is not of a sporty disposition, it is likely that his offspring will be similarly inept on any fields of dreams. This is where Dad's performance in the hundred metres egg-and-spoon race matters.

If Dad's children have done themselves some justice and at least not come in last, then Dad must aim to equal this achievement, if not beat it. Your children will enjoy seeing you as a winner as long as they don't see themselves as losers.

If, however, they are losers, then Dad, tempted though he might be to show them how it's done, must also lose. He must throw the fight, rig the game, snaffle the odds. In the last five yards, roared on by the crowd – all the Mums and Dads, children, teachers, governors and dinner ladies – no one else in sight, the finish tape taut and tempting, Dad must stumble, the spoon must wobble and the egg must fall. He must walk away from the sports field with the words of Marlon Brando ringing in his ears – yes, Dad coulda been a contender.

Dad does this for his child. So that they can both be losers together. If Sports Day included video games it would be a whole different story.

I've been training all year for this... and this time I will rule victorious, Oh yes, this time the Egg and Spoon race is *mine!*

Mum likes having them around and it's important for the kids to see them. But he has no way of controlling whether they, at a basic level, get on. They may have decided before the children came along, before the wedding, before any thought of a wedding even, that he just wasn't the right one for their daughter.

The simplest way of avoiding problems with in-laws is to avoid the in-laws themselves

This is not to say that a determined Dad can never win over sceptical in-laws. Sometimes he can; sometimes he can't.

So what to do? The simplest way of avoiding problems with in-laws is to avoid the in-laws themselves. Go out. Every time Mum says that her Mum and Dad are coming round, Dad can disappear.

The shed and the allotment are good if you want to present an active, useful-type-of-chap front, the pub if you don't care. It's an easy-to-use strategy, but it cannot be employed every time or it will be too obvious what's going on.

Avoiding in-laws inside the house (by moving from one room to another) is not recommended. So, when you have to be in the presence of your other family, when

there is no escape, then the one central guiding tenet is … do not lose your temper.

No matter how goaded, provoked or patronised a Dad feels, if he loses his rag with the in-laws lasting damage may occur. Dad might not be that bothered if he upsets people who annoy him, but Mum will be, and Dad will end up feeling guilty if he exposes the bairns to any edgy family confrontation.

In the case of extreme emergency only, Dad should hand over to Mum. They are her parents, she can deal with them.

Look, I don't care if you are my mother in-law, I will fight you to the death!

Monday | Tuesday | Wednesday | Thursday | Friday | Saturday | Dad day

How to Shop

Dad shops in a number of ways. For himself, with the exception of clothes, like the wandering hunter-gatherer he is, he shops best alone.

Car spares, electronics, gardening equipment and tools, he doesn't need anyone else and is faster and more successful in the solitary hunt.

For his clothes he is best off taking Mum with him. As long as Dad doesn't let her get fancy, Mum is a sound adviser. She will make you get new slippers but stop you from buying either the cheapest cardboard pumps which are excellent value, or the jewel-encrusted Roller-Pimp Training Slipper. They cost a bomb, but they do play MP3s.

Shopping for the kids is likewise something that Mum should probably be involved with. Dad's role here, right from the early days in

Mothercare, is to agree thoughtfully with Mum's choice and get his wallet out at the till.

This getting out the wallet can often, ironically, be the enjoyable part of shopping for Mum with Mum.

Buying a new dress or shoes or a coat or anything where the High Street offers Mum an almost infinite number of choices, can be a difficult experience for many Dads.

Sitting on the threadbare chair outside the ladies' changing rooms in Debenhams for forty minutes at a stretch can be frustrating and boring. A sensible Dad will take some reading matter, or a pencil and pad on which to write lists or draw conservatory designs to nullify the effects of the boredom.

You little swine!
Come back here
with my doughnuts!

How to Handle Teenagers

Teenagers are even harder to handle than toddlers. And they stay up later so you have to deal with them for longer stretches. Young children understand that they are not yet adults; teenagers have no such ability.

You might think Dad would do well to remember his own teenage times. But perhaps not. If he really does some serious remembering, he might end up never trusting or feeling that he knows his children at all.

Teenagers are approaching adulthood and its attendant balancing of freedom and responsibility. They start to want to experience the ways of the grown-ups – sex, cars, drink – things many adults struggle to control throughout their lives, so teenagers have no chance.

Like adults they want and need independence, but like children they are still in the business of testing boundaries. Sometimes they don't just test the boundaries, they drive stolen high-performance sports cars right through them while screeching like the demented offsprogs of a hyena and a banshee. What to do with them?

Pregnancy

Pregnancy is usually something wonderful and precious. But not always. The words teenage and pregnancy belong in tut-tutting news stories in tabloids and gossip magazines.

As a Dad you can't help knowing that the world-altering sacrifices and responsibilities that a baby brings sit somewhat uneasily with the kind of lifestyle teenagers enjoy. You need to make sure you instil an absolute dread of causing pregnancy or being pregnant into your sons and daughters.

If it doesn't work, or you forget, then get ready to deal with some serious life stuff. Whatever dire reproductive states your offspring may drive themselves to, Dad will need to stay calm. A way will be found. Babies make sure of that. Calmness and pragmatism are the keys. Dad does not want to drive his youngsters away.

Arrest

Being telephoned by the police to be informed that Son X or Daughter Y has been arrested is something that a surprising number of Dads experience. And a not unequally surprising number of Dads, once they arrive at the police station, think, *Oh yeah, I remember this place.*

For those Dads who may be strangers to the penal system, there are a few things to bear in mind. If it's a first offence – shoplifting, drunk and disorderly, trading in endangered species – the long arm of the law will probably want to push your child back to you with a caution and a kind of *Get this amateur out of here* frown.

Go along with their *You won't be so lucky next time* homilies. Do not smile when reunited with your young adult; do not speak on the car journey home; save the disappointment speech for at least a day or two while the child stews; adopt an attitude of barely concealed rage and contempt. It should work on redeemable sorts.

If it's a ninth offence and your child greets you in the interview room with an offensive hand gesture, then there's something rotten in the state of Dad. Either it's your fault or it's not your fault; the solution is the same.

If the child is at an age where he or she is legally entitled to leave home, this might be good. For a year or two. You can get back together over a pizza when things have calmed down.

If the child is not of an age to fly the nest, there is only one solution – go on one of those TV shows where a bunch of experts deconstruct your family's lives and rebuild you as more efficiently functioning human beings. Plus you get to be notorious for a while.

The police, you say? No, I'm sorry officer, he is not *my* son... He is adopted.

PART TEN

A

Where are all the answers?

Ask Dad

Ask Dad

For the purposes of 'science-like' enquiry, a specially selected Random Dad (with impeccable credentials) was placed in a large, boring room with thirty children of varying ages who were invited to ask him any questions they wanted. The results are a mixture of the illuminating and the enlightening.

Harriet, aged six, asked:
What is a rainbow?

Dad said: *You've asked a very interesting question. And fortuitously I know the answer. A rainbow only happens when it is sunny and raining at the same time, doesn't it? So, sunshine plus rain equals rainbow.*

The reason that a rainbow is lots of different colours is that sunshine is made up of lots of different colours. But you can only see them when it's raining. Why is it curved? It's curved because ... light's ... bendy?

Gail, aged five, asked:
Where does the sun go?

Dad said: *It doesn't really go anywhere. In our experience, in terms of what we see, in a poetic sense, if you like, it does go. The end of the day, darkness, the sleep of humanity, its nightmares and dreams, the fluctuation between the great polarity that dominates our existence. Yes, in some senses, the sun goes.*

Actually, the world is turning and for a few hours we are just the wrong side of the world to see it. I'd like to give you a follow-up question, Gail, but I've made myself feel a bit dizzy. Just a second.

Samantha, aged three, asked:
Where do babies come from?

Dad said: *I don't know. I've been wondering that. Have you asked your mother? She said a baby grows from a seed? That doesn't sound very likely to me. You were a baby quite recently – can you remember where you came from? Yes, it is hard to remember. Oh, yes, they are lovely shoes.*

Darren, aged eight, asked:
What is it like being drunk?

Dad said: *You're eight and you're asking me? Well, if you really don't know already, there are different sorts of being drunk. You drink a few beers and you can be tiddly, tipsy or merry, and that's good fun.*

You drink a few more beers and you can be sozzled, juiced, trousered or well oiled, and that is good fun too.

You keep drinking those beers and you can be bombed, wrecked, stewed, smashed, hammered or pickled, and then it's not quite such good fun.

And if you manage to keep drinking you can be out of order, well out of order or unconscious, and that's no fun at all. But I still think you know all this already. Am I right? Am I?

Jane, aged eleven, asked:
Who invented money?

Dad said: *What a brilliant question. You're probably some sort of wunderkind, aren't you? Who invented money? Beats me. Wish I had. I'd be pretty rich by now, eh? Wow.*

I've never been asked that before. Are your parents teachers or something? My children never asked me that. Definitely a top notch question. If you're ever up for adoption, here's my card.

Wayne, aged thirteen, asked:
Why can't children drive cars?

Dad said: *Children do drive cars. Every time I'm on the roads there seem to be children driving cars wherever I look. They just happen to be children aged between seventeen and thirty.*

You just have to wait your turn. Why not try go-karting? Children can do that. Go-karts are just cars without shells. And being a car owner is just too expensive for most kids. Don't even think about driving a car until you've got a job. Possibly two.

Jake, aged seven, asked:
Why are people different colours?

The simple answer, Jake, is that people's colour depends where they come from, or where their families came from. Pink people come from Europe, brown people come from India, very brown people come from Africa. Or their Mummies and Daddies did.

There is a more complicated answer to do with geography and sunlight and vitamin A and melanin. But I don't really understand it. The thing to know is that you can't tell what people are like from their colour – people don't choose the colour of their skin, eyes or hair. Occasionally you have to factor in jaundice.

Tarquin, aged twelve, asked:
Why don't boys wear dresses?

Dad said: *The thing about your question is that I feel I should know why you are asking before I answer it. You might just be asking out of a mild curiosity, having observed one of life's anomalies; or you might be looking for me to persuade or dissuade you from something you've been thinking about for a while.*

I know answering a question with a question is not generally the done thing, but in response to your enquiry – does it matter?

Stephanie, aged eight, asked:
Why do I hate people?

Dad said: *You don't hate people. No you don't … Calm down … No, you don't hate everyone … Come on … Here's a hankie … Okay, it's a tissue … There … See? It's not so terrible, is it?*

Look. Life can be difficult sometimes. We have to try to balance what we want with what other people want. And that's not always easy. If things don't go the way you want, then it's only natural to feel bad. But you won't feel bad for ever.

Try to think nice thoughts. Think about the things you like … Yes, I'm sure there's a sweet shop near here. Yes, horses are nice. They are a good thing to think about.

Ian – The runt of the litter, and no taller than
5 foot 8 inches, Ian has never knowingly filled a
shirt. Midlands based, but with a southern twinge
to his accent, he likes to travel to work in a British-
built car and would never consider playing squash.
Or any other racket sports. Although prone to
constipation, when buying his own toilet paper
will almost always choose waxed.

Terry, aged six, asked:
Why don't women have moustaches?

Dad said: *Terry, my man, you have a lot to learn. Some women do have moustaches. They tend not to have beards though. How your hair grows is down to hormones, which are like chemicals in your body, and men have chemicals that make them grow beards and women don't.*

It's really so you can be sure who is a man and who is a woman. If you're going to ask why men shave – I don't know. For my money, a lustrous beard is a beautiful addition to any face.

Sean, aged eight, asked:
Where do babies come from?

Dad said: *This one again. Well, a lad your age, you probably have some idea already. Have the older boys told you something in the playground? They have? And you want me to tell you if it's true.*

I bet what they told you sounds possible but incredibly horrible. It's true. Forget about it for a couple of years though. Between now and you growing a beard, there is lots of time to get used to crazy things.

Laura, aged four, asked:
Why does Uncle Peter smell like burning?

Dad said: *I don't know Uncle Peter. For all I know he may be some kind of pyromaniac. But I suspect he is probably a smoker. Smoking is something you can do when you grow up. It makes you look big and cool, but it kills you.*

My advice is to get your parents to agree to giving you five hundred pounds if you don't smoke a cigarette before your twenty-first birthday. Stay healthy and make money. I know you're only four, but it's as well to plan ahead.

Emma, aged seven, asked:
Why aren't there dinosaurs any more?

Dad said: *There are three answers to your question. The first is that there are still lots of dinosaurs everywhere. All the dinosaurs turned into birds a long time before you were born. So the sky is full of dinosaurs.*

The second answer is that they all died because the world got too cold or too hot for them.

The third answer is that there are some proper big dinosaurs still alive. They live on an island near Costa Rica with David, no Dicky, Attenborough.

Carl, aged ten, asked:
Why do some families have more children than others?

Dad said: *Good question, young man. The answer is that lots of things affect how many children there are in a family. I mean, it's sociology, isn't it? Demographics, relative wealth, health care, culture, religion.*

It's big stuff. You're asking a big question. And then there's just luck. Take as an example the niece of this bloke at work, Gus. His niece … Where's he gone? Where did that boy go?

Gemma, aged four, asked:
Why do pets die?

Dad said: *And not only pets. No, what I mean to say is that pets have different lives. They live here for a while and then they die and their spirits go to Heaven. Yes, like Auntie Hilary.*

Up in Heaven pets get to play around and have fun for ever. What do you think, Gemma? Think I could get a coffee round here? No, I don't think they have school in Heaven.

Hailey, aged six, asked:
Why do people go to work?

Dad said: *The bitter truth, Hailey, my young friend, is that not everybody goes to work. There are people who can't find a job and they want to work. Then there are people who go to work but don't want to. Then there are people who don't work and don't want to work.*

The key ingredient in all this is money. If you haven't got any money you need to work; if you have lots of money you don't. What does your Dad do? A film star? Really? What's his name? Yes, I saw that one. *He's your Dad? Wow. Well, all that stuff I just told you? You don't need to know it.*

Russell, aged nine, asked:
Why do people get old?

Dad said: *You're hitting a nail on its head there, Russell. And you're opening up a philosophical can of worms with that nail. Why do people get old? Processes corrupt, stuff degenerates, everything decays, it doesn't really matter.*

What you're actually asking is whether you will ever be able to accept life's icy background music – the ticking of the clock, the blur of the seasons, the lines yet to appear on your face, your mortality.

Am I right? No. You just want to know why people get old. Well, don't worry, Russell, by the time you're old they'll have cured it and you'll be able to live for ever. Yeah, cool.

Alice, aged three, asked:
Why do people tell lies?

Dad said: *If you think about it, young lady, you probably already know the answer to that question. Why do you* tell lies*? Are you sure? Never? Never ever? No, don't cry. There's no need to cry. Lord above. I didn't say you were a liar … No I didn't … I'm not calling you a liar, I'm merely contradicting you … It's not the same thing at all.*

Gavin, aged eleven, asked:
Why are there wars?

Dad said: *I don't know. It seems like everyone has to hate someone. If you figure this one out, let me know.*

Megan, aged three, asked:
Why can't I have a puppy?

Dad said: *You might be able to have a puppy, but perhaps not just yet. Puppies need looking after and you're not quite old enough to take care of one right now. Maybe in a few years or so. Yes, the same goes for a rabbit. Yes, and a guinea pig. Yes, and a hamster. Yes, and a pony. And the same for a dinosaur.*

Mavis, aged nine, asked:
Why can't I have the same trainers as my friends?

Dad said: *There are a couple of ways of approaching this. There might be a very simple reason for you not being able to have the same trainers as your friends. Your parents might not have the money to pay for them. Or the reasons could be more complicated.*

They might have the money but need it to buy other things – fish fingers, bananas, washing-up liquid. They might have the money but think that the trainers are not very nice and that they wouldn't look good on you. They might just want you to know that you don't have to do everything your friends do or have everything they have.

Which ones do you want anyway? Show me a picture. Oh, they're awesome. No, you're right – they're cool. They'd definitely suit you. You should ask your parents to get you those. Do they do them in a size ten, do you think?

Janice, aged eleven, asked:
Why are boys so stupid?

Dad said: *I don't want to depress you, but you might find yourself asking that question not infrequently throughout your life. Not infrequently means quite often. Yes, I should have said that. Yes, it's probably because I'm a man.*

The thing is, Janice, that eventually, although a long time after girls, boys stop being stupid and can even end up being reasonable. Don't worry too much about it. In a few years they will stop seeming quite so stupid and start to seem amusing and even … interesting.

I don't expect you to believe me. But that's what happens.

Kirk, aged ten, asked:
Will I ever like my sister?

Dad said: *Yes, you will. Probably. There are no guarantees, my friend. The chances are that the reasons you don't like your sister at the moment will disappear. You probably fight over who has what and who gets attention when.*

Once you're all grown up you'll have your own life and your own things and you won't need so much attention. She did what? No. Oh, no. That makes things very different. Yes. Did they? Well, I suppose that's what social workers are for.

Steven, aged six, asked:
Will my Dad ever be able to play football?

Dad said: *No, Steven, he won't. But don't worry about that. Because I know for a fact that your Dad can do things that nobody else's Dad can. I don't know what they are. You'll have to find out.*

James, aged fourteen, asked:
Where do babies come from?

Dad said: *Don't pretend to me that you don't know. You should concentrate your thinking on how to stop babies coming from wherever it is they come from. Off with you.*

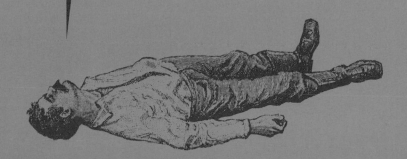

PART ELEVEN

Dad's Recipes

Yummy.

Dad's Recipes

Historically, the kitchen is hostile turf for Dads. It is perfumed with potpourri, full of French words like *flambé, fricassé* and *mayonnaise* and is the indisputable fortress of Mrs Dad. However, there have been a few who have braved this enemy ground, stared danger in the face, and managed to rustle up beautiful and tasty snacks. What follows is a compendium of their soon to be famous work. Salute these heroes; they live in glory.

Bruce Bomb

Ingredients:

1 x slice of Ham – M&S Honey-Roast Ham a must, failing that any of the thicker 'faux-gammons' variety will do.

1 x large spoonful of Cheddar Cheese Coleslaw

1 x large gherkin

1 x smothering of Honey Mustard

Method:

Lay out ham, smear even coating of mustard, slap on generous layer of CCC, use gherkin as bolster, role into vaguely cylindrical shape. Inhale.

Founded:

James Bruce during half-time break at home alone while watching 1999 FA Cup final.

Laziness factor: 6/10

Scotch Surprise

Ingredients:

1 x large Scotch Egg (party eggs will not do)

1 x tub of taramasalata

Method:

Remove Scotch Egg from two-pack (eat other egg while preparing). Remove lid from tub. Carefully slice remaining Scotch egg in two. Take largest, flattest knife from drawer and add the largest amount of tara per square inch of egg possible – repeat.

Founded:

A crossover snack of incredible provenance – the old meeting the new in spectacular style when, in the summer of 1985, at the height of the Greek culinary invasion of Britain, the combination is accidentally discovered by a bored father in Islington, North London.

Laziness factor: 8/10

Le Pie Royale au Lait

Ingredients:

1 x large Pork Pie (must be Melton Mowbray)

1 x small pot of French 'Dijon' mustard

1 x pint chilled full-fat milk

Method:

Remove pie from butter compartment in door of fridge. Place on small breadboard. Slice pie into 8 equal morceaux, dabbing mustard carefully on to peak of each morceau. Greet each mouthful with a soupçon of milk. Ah, sensationnel.

Founded:

Franck Lebeouf circa 1998 – somewhere in those long hours between the end of training and dinner.

Laziness factor: 9/10

Salmon Crumble

Ingredients:

1 x tin of salmon

1 x bag of ready salted crisps

1 x tinned chopped tomatoes

Method:

Open tins and fold salmon chunks into tomatoes. Shape into salmon shape and decant into baking tray. Shake bag of crisps over 'fish'. Place in oven, pre-heated to gas mark whatever. Leave until brown. Served to family with pride.

Founded:

Ian Barham, on paternity leave, Leeds 1989. Having recently had his first child, Ian has not slept a full night in over three weeks.

Laziness factor: 3/10

The Tower of Power

Ingredients:

1 x minute corner of brown bread

1 x pot of smooth peanut butter

Method:

Using full natural bulk of a mature grown Dad, block the families view of this most clandestine of recipes. Carefully remove 1-inch square piece of BROWN bread from loaf – brown gives far better grip – then teaspoon smooth tower of PB on to square. Drop the load straight into open mouth, chew once and swallow.

Founded:

Graham Samuel in 1971 as part of experiment into ingesting most amount of calories in shortest amount of time.

Laziness rating: 9/10

The Dirty Guacamole

Ingredients:

1 x pot of supermarket Guacamole

Method:

Take index and middle finger and make the shape of a gun. Remove lid from pot (with other hand) and insert 'gun' into pot. Make a quick, clean sweep around the perimeter until the Guac is up to second joint of index. Remove, bend 'gun' into spoon shape and place in mouth.

Founded:

12.35am Tijuana, Pepe Ramirez returns from night out salsaing with his mamacita to discover lone, slighty fizzy pot of Guacamole in fridge. 'Andale, mi tummy estas rumblato'.

Laziness rating: 10/10

The Banana Splat

Sealed With a Hiss

Ingredients:

2 x large banana

1 x canister of whipping cream

1 x box of Ambrosia Devon custard

1 x Dairy Milk bar, large

1 x hundreds and thousands

1 x marachino cherry.

Ingredients:

2 x slice of white toast

2 x raw egg

4 x raw rasher streaky bacon

1 x dollop brown sauce

1 x Breville Sandwich maker

Method:

Slice both bananas into inch-wide slices, deposit in bowl. Open box of custard, deposit in bowl. Break Dairy Milk bar into equal segments, deposit in bowl. Spray on pyramid of whipping cream then sprinkle generously with hundreds and thousands. Lavish with cherry. Shovel into mouth with dessert spoon.

Method:

Insert 1 slice of white toast into Breville, crack two eggs . Use large knife to salvage any overspill back on to bread base. Delicately glue rashers of bacon into egg mixture in Union Jack motif, plop brown sauce into cross hairs, depress remaining slice o' white bread on to top. Clip top of Breville into place. Cook until edible.

Founded:

Sunday afternoon, in the 4.30 dessert window, by Sammy Barker, licensed solicitor and father of three.

Founded:

Saturday morning hangover moment of Breville May Care results in this most surprising of breakfast treats.

Laziness rating: 4/10

Laziness rating: 5/10

Epilogue

So there it is. The Book of Dad. The whys, the wherefores, the hows and the whens. The big fajita, the cookie cutter, the master-blaster. The Daddy.

And what have we learned? That the life of Dad is one heck of a journey, one zoomy roller-coaster trip, an upside-down parabola, the trajectory of a stone thrown into the wind, an arrow fired at the sun. Yes indeed, it would seem that Dad is some adventure.

Lest we forget, Dad is a spiritual endeavour too – a life-creating, life-affirming, life-questioning pursuit. It makes ordinary men great and great men superhuman. It makes you cry, hoot, swear, giggle, shout, chortle, scream, laugh, shriek … and then love. It is what you make of it, and what it makes of you.

And then, one day, it's over. The flock flies the coop. The shepherd is left bereft.

And yet he isn't. They will be back, most likely more than he thought possible.

There will be false starts, money stuff, broken hearts. Once that door closes something happens and being Dad becomes part nostalgia. With luck another role waits in the future:

Grandad. The King of Dad.